Family Lineage Healing

Pain, Patterns, Trauma, and Emotions

By

Dr. Alda Sainfort

and are the property of owned by the owners themselves, not affiliated with this document.

Dedication

In honor of my mother, Gislaine Hilaire, my most beloved and Sidi Muhammad al-Jamal, The Guide of The Shadulliyah Sufi Way. May peace and blessings be upon their spirits, souls, and secrets.

Acknowledgment

I want to express my deepest gratitude to my father, Walvidace Hilaire, my dearest beloved husband, Emmanuel Sainfort, and my wonderful children: Maggie Garcia, Majnheiv, and Majnisharah Sainfort; I could not have undertaken this journey without their support.

I want to thank my granddaughter Neomi Alda Garcia for bringing so much joy to my life; my brothers: David, Emmanuel, Joel, Ronald, and Jude Hilaire; my sister Islaine Sainvil (Lainy); my sisters-in-law: Jeanne Angelaire Leveille, Jeanine Hilaire, Anjelet Hilaire, Maggie Alexis, Natasha Joseph, Erica Laurent, and my brother-in-law Marc Sainvil.

I would also like to thank my nieces, nephews, extended families, my neighbors and friends, my Sufi teachers, and my supporters, all of those who have participated in my family lineage healing retreats in the US /or abroad, and those who have inspired me to write this book and contributed positively.

Table of Contents

Introduction

There is a deep and undeniable connection between our ancestors and us that many of us are disconnected from. For some, the past is shrouded in mystery, leaving us feeling lost and isolated. For others, trauma, abuse, or adoption has left us struggling to find our place in the world. But no matter our circumstances, our ancestors' DNA flows through our veins, and their experiences are imprinted on our souls in every aspect: physical, emotional, mental, and spiritual.

This book aims to bring awareness to the importance of family lineage and ancestral healing and to honor those who came before us. Whether we know our family story or not, our ancestors' legacies continue to influence us in ways we may not even realize. The pain and trauma they endured and the blessings they passed down shape our lives profoundly.

For those with PTSD, birth-related trauma, in-utero trauma, adult trauma, or childhood abuse and neglect, the journey toward healing often begins with exploring our family history. Understanding where we come from can unravel the patterns that may hold us back. As a result, we can develop greater compassion for ourselves and our ancestors and break the cycle of pain passed down through generations.

Searching for their roots can be an emotional and transformative journey for those adopted as infants. Piecing together their family tree and genealogy allows them to discover more about their past and gain a greater sense of belonging. This book offers a roadmap toward deeper understanding and connection for others who are disconnected from their lineage or do not know how important it is to honor their roots.

For those who suffer from spiritual harm, such as the loss of cultural identity or the suppression of ancestral practices, family lineage healing enables them to reconnect with their heritage and reclaim their identity. For those who suffer from genetic, inherited, or generational trauma, such as violence, rape, slavery, or the Holocaust, the process of family lineage repair helps them to break the cycle of pain and create a legacy of healing and growth for future generations.

It's important to acknowledge that family lineage healing can be challenging. Each person's journey will be unique, and the process may look different depending on the individual's circumstances and cultural background. Nevertheless, it requires us to confront painful memories and emotions and to be willing to delve deep into our family history. It also requires us to approach this process with compassion and understanding rather than judgment or blame.

However, the benefits of lineage healing are profound. Understanding and honoring our ancestors helps us to create a deeper sense of belonging in the world. It empowers us better to understand ourselves and our place in the world and develop a sense of purpose and direction in life. It also helps us break free from inherited patterns and beliefs that no longer serve us and create a legacy of healing and growth for future generations.

This book is for anyone hungry for belonging and connection to their roots. It's for those ready to embark on a journey of self-discovery and healing and willing to confront the challenges and rewards that come with it. It's for those who want to honor their ancestors and create a brighter future for themselves and their descendants.

In conclusion, family lineage healing is a powerful and transformative process that helps us to connect with our roots, heal inherited wounds, and fully embody our gifts and potential. It requires courage, patience, and self-compassion, but it's a journey that can ultimately lead to greater peace, purpose, and joy. This book is a guide towards understanding the importance of healing family lineage, honoring those who came before us, and a roadmap towards a brighter and more connected future.

What is Family Lineage?

Family lineage refers to the ancestry or lineage of a person, tracing their ancestors and descent from previous generations. It can also refer to the study of genealogy, which investigates and traces family lineages, usually by examining birth, death, marriage, and other relevant records. The idea of family lineage is to understand one's ancestry and cultural heritage and can provide a sense of identity and history. Additionally, it helps individuals understand the transmission of genetic traits and medical history within their family.

Family lineage opens the door and connections with ancestors across generations. It is the study of family history and the tracing of the lineage of one's family, including forebears, descendants, and relatives.

Family lineage includes information such as the names, dates of birth and death, and relationships between family members, often compiled through examining historical records, such as census data, birth certificates, and death certificates. It also provides insights into cultural heritage and a sense of identity for individuals. In addition, it better explains family traditions, values, and customs passed down through generations.

Why Is the Understanding of Family Lineage Critical?

The understanding of family lineage is essential for several reasons, including:

Sense of identity and belonging

Understanding family lineage provides a strong sense of identity and belonging. Knowing one's ancestry and family history offers a sense of belonging by connecting individuals to their heritage, culture, and traditions. Often, the knowledge of the lives, experiences, and challenges faced by one's ancestors gives a deeper understanding of one's identity and place in the world.

It generates a more profound connection to one's heritage and cultural background. This creates a sense of belonging as individuals feel a part of something greater than themselves and feel connected to the history and traditions of their ancestors.

Knowing one's family lineage also gives individuals a sense of identity, as it provides a connection to where they come from and the people and cultural influences that contribute to shaping who they are. This gives individuals a deeper understanding of themselves and a stronger connection to their personal and cultural history.

Additionally, family lineage helps individuals discover their cultural roots and give them a sense of pride in their heritage, including learning about their cultural traditions, language, and customs. This contributes to their self-esteem and helps them develop a stronger sense of identity and belonging within their community and the world.

Thus, understanding one's family lineage is vital to building a solid identity and belonging. It brings a sense of connection to the past and provides individuals with a foundation for their future.

Cultural heritage

Family lineage offers insight into cultural heritage, including traditions, values, and beliefs passed down through generations.

Cultural heritage is an essential aspect of identity and can significantly shape one's beliefs, values, and perspectives. Family lineage gives valuable insight into this cultural heritage by tracing the history and traditions of one's ancestors.

Knowing about one's family's traditions, such as religious customs, cultural celebrations, and traditional cuisine, further accentuates the importance for individuals to understand the cultural values passed down through generations. This gives individuals a deeper appreciation for their cultural heritage and helps them maintain a connection to their roots.

In addition, it also brings insight into the historical and political events that have shaped culture and how they have influenced its values and beliefs. For example, knowing about a family's immigration history or experiences during significant events such as wars can lead one to a deeper understanding of how cultural heritage has evolved.

Furthermore, preserving cultural heritage is crucial to maintaining identity and belonging. By learning about and preserving their cultural heritage, individuals help to ensure that their cultural traditions and values are passed down to future generations.

Family lineage is a valuable tool for understanding and preserving cultural heritage. By tracing the history and traditions of one's ancestors, individuals gain a deeper appreciation for their cultural heritage and maintain a connection to their roots.

Historical context

Understanding one's family lineage and history provides insight into historical events and how they may have impacted one's ancestors. Personal and family history is deeply intertwined with the broader historical context.

For example, if one of your ancestors was alive during a war, they may have been directly impacted by the events of that conflict. In addition, they may have served in the military, been a refugee, or been directly affected by the war. Studying the history of that conflict helps you gain a deeper understanding of your ancestor's experiences and how the events of that time shaped their life.

Similarly, if your ancestors lived during a time of significant social or political change, such as World War II, the American Civil Rights Movement, or the Industrial Revolution, their experiences and perspectives offer valuable insights into the historical context of that time. Examining the history of these events enables you to understand better the world that your ancestors lived in and how it shaped their experiences.

Tracing your family history and learning about the historical context in which your ancestors lived allows you to gain a deeper appreciation of your personal and family story and the broader history of the world.

Genetic inheritance

Genetics refers to studying an individual's genetic makeup and the potential impact of inherited genes on their health. Understanding family lineage empowers you to understand their genetic inheritance, including any genetic conditions present in their family, and assesses your risk for developing similar conditions. This knowledge helps you make informed decisions about your health and well-being.

Genetic conditions or diseases can sometimes run in families and be passed down from generation to generation. Therefore, researching the genetic conditions present in a family exposes you to your family's medical history and your potential risk for certain conditions.

For example, if a genetic condition is common in your family, you may choose to get tested for carrier status or undergo genetic counseling. This allows you to understand your chances of passing the condition on to your children and make decisions about starting a family.

It's also important to note that many genetic conditions are inherited in a dominant or recessive pattern, which helps to predict the likelihood of passing on the condition to future generations. However, some genetic disorders may arise spontaneously and not be inherited, so it is always a good idea to seek the advice of a healthcare professional.

Medical history

Family lineage provides essential information about an individual's medical history, which can be important for determining the likelihood of inheriting certain conditions or diseases.

A family's medical history offers valuable information about an individual's likelihood of inheriting certain conditions or diseases.

For example, suppose several members of an individual's family have a history of heart disease. In that case, the individual may have an increased risk of developing heart disease due to a genetic predisposition. This information encourages the individual to make informed decisions about their lifestyle and healthcare, such as changing their diet and exercise habits or discussing preventive measures with their healthcare provider.

In addition to providing information about the likelihood of inheriting certain conditions, a family's medical history presents essential information about other health-related factors, such as the age at which certain conditions develop, the presence of multiple conditions in the same individual, and any treatments that have been effective in the past. This information helps create a personalized healthcare plan that considers an individual's unique medical history and needs.

It is important to note that a family's medical history is just one factor influencing an individual's health. Other factors, such as lifestyle, environment, and personal behavior, also play a role in determining an individual's overall health. Therefore, considering their family medical history and other relevant factors allows individuals to make informed decisions about their health and work with their healthcare provider to develop a personalized healthcare plan.

Genealogy research

Studying family lineage can be fascinating, as it allows individuals to learn their ancestry and more about their family's history.

Genealogy research can be a gratifying hobby. It involves tracing one's family history and ancestry to learn as much as possible about one's family lineage. This includes researching historical records, such as birth certificates, marriage licenses, and census data, and connecting with living relatives to gather information and family stories.

One of the main appeals of genealogy research is the sense of discovery that comes with learning about one's ancestors. People may be surprised that they have a rich and diverse family history with roots in different countries and cultures. In addition, through genealogy research, individuals uncover stories of strength and perseverance in the face of adversity and learn about their ancestors' contributions to their communities and the world.

Genealogy research also permits individuals to understand better the context in which their ancestors lived, including historical events, social and political changes, and cultural trends. This provides valuable insights into the world that shaped their ancestors and helped to bring the past to life.

In addition to the personal benefits, genealogy research is also a way to connect with others with similar interests. Many genealogy enthusiasts join local or online groups, attend conferences and workshops, and participate in other events that present opportunities to network and learn from others who are also passionate about family history research.

Overall, genealogy research presents a deeper understanding of one's family history, a sense of belonging, identity, and a connection to the past.

What Is the Importance of Family Lineage to Family Lineage Healing?

Family lineage is intrinsic to family lineage healing because it provides a sense of belonging, identity, and connection to the past. In addition, when people can trace their family lineage, they can learn about their ancestors and their experiences. This knowledge enables individuals better to understand themselves and their place in the world and provides a deeper appreciation for the sacrifices and struggles of their ancestors.

Additionally, tracing one's family lineage uncovers any unresolved issues or traumas that have been passed down from generation to generation. For example, suppose a family has a history of addiction, mental health issues, or other forms of trauma. In that case, understanding the root cause of these problems empowers individuals to develop strategies for healing and moving forward.

Finally, connecting with one's family lineage helps build community and strengthen family bonds. When people can share their family stories and history, they form a deeper connection and appreciation for each other, which help to heal any rifts or conflicts within the family.

Tracing one's family lineage and engaging in family lineage healing positively impact an individual's sense of identity, well-being, and relationships with others.

Epigenetic Science

Our current scientific knowledge of our DNA is limited in fully comprehending our true identity. However, recent research reveals that our genetic program is not fixed and can change based on the choices we make throughout our lives. Depending on our environment and decisions, our DNA can express itself in various ways, which is referred to as genetic plasticity.

When born, we come with presets (default settings) that help us survive and navigate basic human relationships and purposes. However, these settings are flexible and can be upgraded and expanded beyond these basics to reach our full potential.

Contrary to what we have been taught, our DNA is not set in stone, and the legacies of our ancestors do not bind us.

We have the capacity to self-regulate and heal both physically and emotionally, as well as to access deep intuition on demand.

Epigenetics helps explain how cells, even identical ones, behave differently when exposed to varying environments. As human beings, we are made up of these cells, and when we encounter harmful factors like a poor diet, stress, or substance abuse, our DNA may respond with negative outcomes, such as disease. However, we have the ability to take control of our lives and change our fate. We do not have to be defined by our circumstances or inherit negative patterns. We can unlock our genetic potential and achieve optimal well-being by prioritizing our physical, mental, and spiritual health.

This is where the understanding of the concept of ancestral energy becomes crucial. Its influence on our lives is rooted in many ancient traditions and belief systems. According to these traditions, our ancestors continue to exist in a spiritual realm even after their physical bodies have perished. They continue to carry their unique energy and consciousness, which can affect the lives of their descendants.

Although ancestral energy is often associated with negativity, it can also have positive effects. Ancestors who lived a positive and intentioned life can leave behind a positive legacy and offer help in various forms. They can provide guidance and support during difficult times or offer insights into important decisions that need to be made. Furthermore, ancestral spirits who care for us may appear in our dreams to give instructions or warn us about danger, acting as protectors and advisors. In some instances, the influence of cultivated ancestors can extend beyond personal guidance and have a broader impact on the world. Many great artists and spiritual leaders have been inspired by the wisdom and creativity of their ancestors. For example, Shakespeare, Homer, Goethe, and Dante's works draw heavily on ancestral knowledge and inspiration.

It is fascinating to note that the final section of Dante's Divine Comedy was lost after his death, but it was later discovered by his son. Legend has it that Dante's son was visited by his father in a dream and was given instructions on where to locate the missing manuscript. This tale is frequently mentioned as an illustration of how our ancestors' wisdom can significantly impact our lives, even after they have passed away.

When the ancestral energy is negative, it can cause significant problems for their descendants, affecting their behavior and thought patterns. This negative ancestral energy can further generate epigenetic tags of mental, emotional, and physical illnesses, anxieties, PTSD, and fears, which can be passed down through generations. This is because our energy bodies are interconnected, and the energy of our ancestors can affect us even when they have passed away. However, we are not powerless in the face of this energy. We can take several steps to protect ourselves and cultivate positive energy in our lives.

One of the most effective ways to protect ourselves from negative ancestral energy is through spiritual practices that focus on energy healing and connecting with positive ancestral energy. Meditation, for instance, is a powerful tool for calming the mind and cultivating inner peace. By meditating regularly, we can learn to tune out the noise of negative ancestral energy and connect with our inner wisdom and guidance.

Energy healing practices such as acupuncture or acupressure can also be beneficial in balancing and harmonizing the energy flow in our bodies. These practices address energy blockages and imbalances caused by negative ancestral energy.

It's also important to cultivate positive energy through healthy habits and positive relationships. Eating a healthy diet, regular exercise, and engaging in hobbies and activities that bring us joy can all help to boost our energy and overall well-being. Building positive relationships with friends and family can also provide a supportive and uplifting environment that counteracts negative ancestral energy.

Finally, it's essential to practice self-awareness and self-care. By understanding our own thought patterns, behaviors, and emotional responses, we can identify areas where negative ancestral energy may be affecting us and take steps to address these issues. This may involve seeking professional help from a therapist or energy healer or simply taking time to rest, reflect, and recharge.

Interestingly, epigenetic tags can pop off when we heal from them. By extension, everybody that descended from that ancestor in an energetic sense also gets the healing; this is like a domino effect.

What Is Family Lineage Healing?

F amily lineage healing is a process of acknowledging, exploring, and healing intergenerational trauma and patterns within families and individuals. It involves identifying and understanding the emotional and psychological scars passed down from generation to generation and working to heal them in oneself and one's family system.

The concept of family lineage healing recognizes that our ancestors' experiences, positive and negative, have a profound impact on our lives and our relationships with others, including patterns of behavior, beliefs, and emotions that are passed down and influence our own lives and the lives of our progenies.

To heal, it is vital first to understand and acknowledge these patterns and then work towards releasing and transforming them. This involves individual self-exploration, family therapy, or other healing modalities that address the root causes of these patterns.

Family lineage healing also involves rituals and practices aimed at honoring and connecting with one's ancestors and releasing negative energies and patterns from the past. This creates a greater sense of peace, connectedness, and wholeness within the family.

Family lineage healing is a practice that seeks to heal the wounds of the past and restore balance to a family's history. It involves looking at the patterns of behavior and beliefs passed down through generations and understanding how they have impacted the family's present. Through this practice, individuals gain insight into their family's history and how it has shaped their lives. It also helps heal past wounds and create a healthier, more balanced family dynamic.

Family lineage healing is a powerful tool for understanding and healing the past. It uncovers our ancestors' stories and experiences and helps us gain valuable insight into how our family's history has shaped our lives. Additionally, it creates a sense of connection and belonging as individuals gain a deeper understanding of their family's history and identity.

Similarly, it is considered a type of spiritual or energy healing that seeks to address and heal the emotional and psychological wounds embedded in our subconscious that are passed down from generation to generation within families. The belief is that trauma and harmful patterns of behavior, thoughts, and emotions within families are unconsciously passed down from one generation to the next and impact the health and well-being of family members.

In family lineage healing, healers use techniques such as purification of attributes with the Divine Names of God, visualization, meditation, affirmations, and other methods to release blocked energy and break negative patterns. In addition, this type of healing often involves exploring one's family history and identifying patterns of trauma or dysfunction that may affect family members' present-day health and well-being. Addressing and healing these negative patterns and traumas allow healers to promote physical, emotional, and spiritual healing for the individual and their family.

In family lineage healing, it is also believed that healing one's wounds and breaking negative patterns influence future generations positively and prevent these patterns from being passed down further. In addition, this type of healing is often seen as a way to honor and respect the ancestors who have come before us and take responsibility for our actions and beliefs impacting future generations.

Lineage issues usually overpoweringly impact our lives, even when unaware of their existence. These issues manifest in our relationships, our career choices, our health, and our overall sense of well-being. Understanding our family's history and lineage enables us to understand how our family's past has shaped our present. This helps us identify patterns of behavior and beliefs passed down through generations and to create healthier, more balanced relationships. Additionally, it generates a sense of connection and belonging as individuals understand their family's history and identity deeper. It also engenders a sense of hope and possibility as individuals become aware of how their family's history has shaped their lives.

We carry inherited impressions of things that happened to our ancestors, dead or alive, which significantly impact our lives, even when unaware of their existence. These impressions manifest in our relationships, our career choices, our health, and our overall sense of well-being. Knowing our family's history and lineage helps us to make more informed decisions and create a healthier, more fulfilling life.

By exploring our family's history, we deeply understand our identity and how our ancestors have influenced our lives. Doing this teaches us about our family's culture, values, and traditions and how these have been passed down through generations. We also know how our family's struggles and successes have shaped our lives. Recognizing our family's history allows us to appreciate our own unique identity and the legacy of our ancestors more.

This recognition is facilitated through collective healing techniques, including therapy, ancestral healing practices, energy healing, bodywork, and other forms of treatment that help address and release the negative patterns and emotions passed down through the generations. The goal is to create a space where individuals can come together and work to heal the collective wound and bring light to the soul.

This process allows individuals to deeply learn their family history and the impact that their ancestors' experiences have had on their own lives. It also works to heal the wounds passed down to them and to release negative patterns and beliefs holding them back. This leads to greater self-awareness, increased resilience, and a greater connection to their family, community, and cultural heritage.

It is indeed the case that the experiences and emotions of our ancestors can have a profound impact on us, even if we are not consciously aware of it. Furthermore, these experiences and feelings can be stored in our DNA and passed down through generations, affecting our thoughts, behaviors, physical health, and well-being.

For example, trauma experienced by our ancestors leads to the intergenerational transmission of trauma. Their experiences are passed down through the generations, affecting future generations' mental and emotional well-being. In addition, ancestral trauma manifests as various psychological issues, such as anxiety, depression, fear, and difficulty forming healthy relationships. This also causes feelings of disconnection from our cultural heritage and sense of belonging.

To heal from ancestral trauma is essential to become more aware of these issues and their impact on our lives. This involves exploring our family history and cultural heritage, connecting with our ancestral roots, and learning about traditional healing practices.

On a deeper level, our ancestors' experiences also influence our sense of identity and belonging. The inability to feel connected to our family lineage or cultural heritage leads to feelings of loss, confusion, and disconnection.

However, it's important to note that we can heal and reclaim our sense of self, even in the face of inherited trauma and disconnection from our lineage. Becoming more aware of our ancestors' experiences and influences helps us better understand ourselves and work towards healing and growth.

Ultimately, healing from ancestral trauma requires deep self-awareness and self-reflection. By becoming more mindful of the experiences and emotions passed down through your family line, you can reclaim a sense of peace and connection with yourself and create a brighter future for future generations.

Disclaimer

Family lineage healing is not a substitute for traditional medical or mental health treatments. It should not be used solely for severe medical or psychological conditions. However, it can be used as a complementary approach to help support overall health and well-being. It is a valuable tool for anyone seeking to improve their health and well-being and those interested in understanding and healing the intergenerational patterns affecting their lives.

The Importance of Family Lineage Healing to the Holistic Health of a Person

Family lineage healing can significantly impact a person's holistic health and well-being. Here are some of the key reasons why family lineage healing is vital for achieving overall health and wellness:

Identifying and addressing inherited patterns

Family lineage healing helps individuals to identify and understand patterns of illness, trauma, and dysfunction that may have been passed down through their family tree. By exploring these patterns and understanding their roots, individuals break the cycle and create new, healthier patterns for themselves and future generations.

In family lineage healing, inherited patterns refer to the traits, behaviors, beliefs, and attitudes passed down from one generation to another within a family. These patterns can be positive, such as a strong work ethic or a love of music, or negative, such as patterns of addiction, abuse, or depression.

Negative patterns that are not addressed cause a ripple effect through generations, with each new generation

21

potentially experiencing more severe symptoms of the underlying issues. For example, a family history of addiction often leads to more severe addiction issues in subsequent generations, or a history of trauma often causes more severe mental health challenges in future generations.

Through family lineage healing, individuals explore their family history and identify negative patterns that may impact their health and well-being. This involves delving into family stories, examining patterns of behavior and relationships, and exploring the emotional and psychological impact of past traumas and events.

Once negative patterns have been identified, family lineage healing allows individuals to break the cycle and create new, healthier patterns for themselves and future generations. This may involve developing new coping mechanisms, setting healthier boundaries, and practicing self-care and self-compassion.

Breaking negative patterns and creating new, healthier ones make individuals experience a better sense of emotional and mental well-being, positively impacting physical health. Additionally, breaking negative patterns creates a positive ripple effect through future generations and helps promote excellent health and well-being for all family members.

Promoting emotional healing

Many patterns of illness and dysfunction are rooted in unresolved emotional trauma or pain from the past. Family lineage healing provides a safe and supportive space to explore and process these emotions, leading to more remarkable emotional healing and well-being.

Family lineage healing presents a unique opportunity to explore and process emotional trauma or pain passed down through the generations. When we carry unresolved emotional trauma from our ancestors, it manifests as patterns of illness, dysfunction, and other life challenges. By bringing these patterns to light and exploring their roots, we will begin to release the emotional pain and find more remarkable emotional healing and well-being.

Through family lineage healing, individuals access a safe and supportive space to process their emotions and better understand themselves and their family history. This involves exploring family dynamics, examining the roles and relationships of ancestors, and reflecting on how these patterns have affected their lives.

One key aspect of family lineage healing is acknowledging and honoring the experiences of ancestors who may have suffered or experienced trauma.

Recognizing their struggles and honoring their resilience make individuals heal and release patterns of pain and dysfunction that have been passed down.

Additionally, family lineage healing creates a sense of empowerment and agency for individuals who may have felt powerless or trapped by their family history. By understanding the roots of inherited patterns, individuals break the cycle and create new, healthier habits for themselves and future generations.

Family lineage healing can be a powerful tool for emotional healing and well-being. Exploring and processing inherited emotional trauma and pain patterns help individuals find greater self-awareness, emotional resilience, and a deeper connection to themselves and their ancestral lineage.

Reducing stress and anxiety

Carrying inherited patterns of illness or trauma creates constant stress and anxiety in our lives. Family lineage healing reduces this stress by addressing the root causes and creating new, healthier patterns that promote relaxation and calm.

Inherited patterns of illness or trauma may be rooted in past experiences of our ancestors but are passed down to us through our genes, behaviors, and even our beliefs. As a result, we may experience stress and anxiety without fully understanding their reasons.

Family lineage healing offers a space to explore and address these patterns, leading to a reduction in stress and anxiety. By understanding our family history and inherited patterns, we will see how these patterns affect our lives and identify specific triggers contributing to our stress and anxiety.

Through family lineage healing, we also learn new techniques for managing stress and anxiety. For example, we may explore mindfulness practices, heart-based/sound healing meditation, relaxation techniques, or other strategies to help us feel calmer and more centered. We may also learn new ways of coping with difficult emotions and challenging situations, helping us feel more in control and less overwhelmed.

By addressing the root causes of our stress and anxiety and learning new strategies for managing these emotions through family lineage healing, we will feel more relaxed and be more at ease in our lives experience; this leads to greater emotional well-being, improved physical health, balance, and harmony.

Improving physical health

Inherited patterns of illness can also directly impact our physical health. Therefore, identifying and addressing these patterns helps to improve overall physical health and well-being.

Inherited patterns of illness influence our physical health in many ways. For example, certain genetic mutations or imbalances increase our risk for specific health conditions. At the same time, other patterns of illness may be related to lifestyle factors or environmental exposures passed down through the generations.

Family lineage healing improves physical health by identifying and addressing these patterns. Through techniques such as genealogy research, ancestral clearing, and epigenetic therapy, we gain a deeper understanding of our family history and the specific patterns of illness that may be affecting us.

Once we have identified these patterns, we can work to address them through various means. For example, we may explore dietary changes, exercise programs, or other lifestyle modifications which help to reduce our risk for specific health conditions. We may also explore alternative therapies, such as acupuncture or energy healing to promote physical healing and well-being.

In addition to these techniques, family lineage healing promotes overall physical health by reducing stress and anxiety. Chronic stress negatively impacts many aspects of our health, including our immune, digestive, and cardiovascular systems. Family lineage healing supports these systems and improves overall physical health by reducing stress and promoting relaxation.

Improving physical health through family lineage healing enables us to experience various benefits, including increased energy, better sleep, and a more robust immune system. We may also experience a reduction in chronic pain and other physical symptoms and an overall improvement in our quality of life.

Therefore, family lineage healing significantly influences our overall health and quality of life by addressing inherited patterns of illness and promoting physical health and well-being. It makes us feel more in control of our health, reduces our risk for specific health conditions, and promotes optimal physical functioning and vitality.

Strengthening relationships

Family lineage healing creates a deeper connection and understanding with family members, including those who have passed on. This brings more substantial, supportive relationships and a greater sense of community and belonging.

Family lineage healing strengthens relationships by promoting a deeper understanding of our family history and dynamics. Through this process, we have a greater appreciation for our ancestors' struggles and challenges and their embodied strengths and qualities.

Exploring our family lineage brings a better knowledge of our history and how it has shaped our beliefs, values, and behaviors. This knowledge helps us develop greater empathy and compassion for family members with different perspectives or experiences.

Additionally, family lineage healing offers an opportunity to connect with family members. By honoring the memory of passed-on generations and acknowledging their contributions to our family, we will feel a sense of connection and support that transcends time and space.

Strengthening relationships through family lineage healing increases emotional support, deeper connections with loved ones, and a greater sense of community and belonging. As a result, we can better navigate complex family dynamics and conflicts and communicate more effectively with our loved ones. Overall, family lineage healing can help to promote greater emotional well-being and healthier relationships within our families.

Creating a sense of purpose and meaning

Exploring and understanding our family history engenders a deeper purpose and meaning. Family lineage healing empowers us to connect with our roots and initiates a sense of continuity and purpose beyond our individual lives.

Exploring our family history through family lineage healing provides a greater sense of connection to our past, present, and future. Again, by understanding our ancestors' experiences and challenges, we will better appreciate our lives and the opportunities and resources available.

In addition, family lineage healing encourages us to identify our unique gifts, talents, strengths, and the values and qualities most important to us. Recognizing and aligning these qualities with our sense of purpose and meaning will create a greater understanding of direction and focus on our lives.

Furthermore, family lineage healing enables us to see ourselves as part of a larger picture, connecting us to a lineage of individuals who have contributed to our family history and left a legacy we can continue to build upon. This promotes a sense of continuity and purpose beyond our individual lives and future generations.

Connecting with our family lineage and exploring our unique gifts and values gives a greater sense of purpose and meaning in our lives, leading to greater fulfillment, satisfaction, and overall well-being.

Family lineage healing helps create a healthier, more fulfilling life for oneself and future generations by exploring and addressing inherited patterns, promoting emotional healing, reducing stress and anxiety, improving physical health, strengthening relationships, and creating a sense of purpose and meaning.

Common Techniques Used in Family Lineage Healing

There are various techniques and approaches used in family lineage healing, and the specific techniques used will depend on the individual healer or practitioner and the client's needs.

Family lineage healing consists of therapeutic approaches to identify and resolve inherited trauma, dysfunction, or illness patterns passed down from generation to generation within a family system. Here are some of the most common techniques used in family lineage healing:

Family Constellations

Family Constellations is a therapeutic approach that uses group work to help individuals connect with their family system's hidden dynamics and unresolved traumas. This technique helps identify and release negative patterns and entanglements, allowing healing.

Family Constellations is a systemic therapeutic approach developed by Bert Hellinger, a German psychotherapist. It is based on the belief that families are systems that are interconnected and influenced by the experiences of their members. This approach aims to reveal and resolve hidden dynamics within family systems that can contribute to problems such as relationship difficulties, mental health issues, and other forms of suffering.

In a Family Constellation session, the client describes their family history, including any significant events or relationships. The therapist then facilitates a group process in which group members are selected to represent different family members or important events. Finally, the client places these "representatives" about one another, often in a spatial arrangement, allowing them to see the dynamics within their family system.

The representatives then experience the emotions, sensations, and thought patterns associated with the person they represent. This process can bring to light hidden patterns or traumas contributing to the client's current issues. The therapist then works with the group to explore and release any negative patterns or entanglements that have been identified.

Family Constellations is a powerful technique that enables individuals to obtain a new perspective on their family history and relationships. By identifying and resolving negative patterns, individuals can experience a sense of release and healing, leading to greater well-being and improved relationships with family members. However, it is important to note that Family Constellations is not a substitute for professional therapy and may not be suitable for everyone.

Ancestral Clearing

The ancestral clearing is a process that involves identifying and releasing limiting beliefs, negative emotions, and unprocessed trauma that have been inherited from one's ancestors. They are imprinted in our DNA and we may be carrying these patterns in our energy field and subconscious mind. This technique can be done through various means, such as meditation, visualization, or energy healing.

Common techniques used in ancestral clearing:

Guided visualization: In this technique, the individual is guided through a visualization exercise where they connect with their ancestors and visualize releasing negative emotions, beliefs, or patterns.

Energetic healing: This involves using various energy-based techniques to clear and balance the individual's energy field and witness the light of the soul.

Affirmations: Affirmations are positive statements repeated to reprogram the subconscious mind. In an ancestral clearing, affirmations release negative beliefs and patterns inherited from one's ancestors.

Forgiveness practice: Forgiveness is a powerful tool for releasing negative emotions and patterns. In an ancestral clearing, individuals may be guided through a forgiveness practice to release resentment or anger towards their ancestors.

Journaling: Journaling is a technique that can help individuals identify any negative beliefs or patterns that may be impacting their lives. By writing down their thoughts and feelings, individuals can gain insight into their subconscious mind and begin to release any negative patterns.

Overall, ancestral clearing is a process of identifying and releasing any negative beliefs, emotions, or patterns that may have been inherited from one's ancestors. By doing so, individuals can remove any energetic blocks impacting their health, relationships, or overall well-being. Ancestral clearing can be a powerful tool for gaining insight into one's family history and ancestry and promoting healing and personal growth.

Genealogy Research

Genealogy research involves exploring one's family tree and tracing the patterns of disease, trauma, and dysfunction that may have been passed down from previous generations. By understanding the historical context of these patterns, individuals can gain insight into how they may affect their lives and how to address them.

Genealogy research can be a valuable technique in family lineage healing. It allows individuals to explore their family history and understand patterns passed down from previous generations.

There are several steps involved in genealogy research as a technique for family lineage healing:

Research: The first step in genealogy research is to gather information about one's ancestors. This can involve collecting birth and death certificates, census records, marriage licenses, and other historical records.

Analysis: Once the information has been collected, the next step is to analyze it and look for patterns and trends. This can involve tracing the history of diseases or conditions that have affected the family, identifying any traumatic events or patterns of dysfunction, and looking for any other commonalities that may be relevant.

Interpretation: After analyzing the information, the next step is to interpret it and gain insight into how these patterns may impact the individual's life. This may involve working with a family lineage healer or therapist to understand how past traumas or patterns affect the individual's health, relationships, safety, or security.

Addressing: Finally, the individual can address any patterns or traumas identified through genealogy research. This may involve techniques like family constellations, inner child work, or energy healing to release negative patterns or emotions impacting their lives.

Overall, genealogy research allows individuals to gain insight into their family history and understand how past events and patterns may impact their lives. By addressing these patterns and traumas, individuals can promote healing and personal growth and break free from negative patterns passed down through the family lineage.

Family Ritual

A family ritual is another technique used in family lineage healing. Family rituals can be used to honor and connect with one's ancestors, such as setting up an altar, lighting candles, or performing ceremonies that acknowledge and heal the past. These rituals allow individuals to feel a sense of connection and support from their ancestral lineage.

Family rituals are a powerful technique in family lineage healing. They can honor and connect with one's ancestors and create a sense of continuity between past, present, and future generations. Family rituals take many forms and can be adapted to suit the needs and preferences of each family.

Here are some ways family rituals are used, depending on cultural, spiritual, and religious background, in family lineage healing:

Creating an altar: An altar can be a home space dedicated to connecting with one's ancestors. This can include photographs, candles, flowers, or other objects that are meaningful to the family.

Lighting candles: Lighting candles represents the Divine Light that shines in darkness, we are not alone, or a way of asking or accepting help from the angels or archangels, and spirit guides; these can be simple and powerful way to honor one's ancestors and connect with their energy. Candles can be burned during a specific time of the day or family gatherings to create a sense of connection and continuity.

Performing ceremonies: Prayers or ceremonies can be performed to mark important milestones, such as birthdays, weddings, or other significant events. In addition, these ceremonies can be adapted to include elements that honor and connect with one's ancestors.

Sharing stories: Sharing stories about one's ancestors can be a powerful way to create a sense of connection and continuity between past and present generations. These stories can be shared during family gatherings or recorded for future generations.

Celebrating cultural traditions: Celebrating cultural traditions can be a way to honor one's ancestry and create a sense of continuity with one's cultural heritage. This can include participating in cultural events or preparing traditional foods.

Family rituals can be a powerful way to connect with and honor one's ancestors, creating a sense of continuity between past, present, and future generations. These rituals can be adapted to suit the needs and preferences of each family and can be used to promote healing and personal growth by acknowledging and healing the past.

Epigenetic Therapy

Epigenetic therapy is an emerging technique in family lineage healing that focuses on identifying and treating genetic mutations and imbalances that may contribute to inherited illness or disease patterns. This approach can be combined with other techniques to support healing on a genetic level. It recognizes that environmental factors, such as diet, lifestyle, and stress, can influence genes, causing gene expression and function changes.

Epigenetic therapy involves a variety of techniques that are designed to support healing on a genetic level, including:

Genetic testing: Genetic testing is used to identify specific genetic mutations or imbalances contributing to inherited patterns of illness or disease. This includes testing for gene mutations associated with certain types of cancer, heart disease, or other conditions.

Nutritional therapy: Nutritional therapy supports healing on a genetic level by providing the body with the nutrients it needs to support optimal gene expression and function. This includes incorporating nutrient-dense foods into the diet and using targeted supplements to support specific genetic pathways.

Lifestyle changes: Lifestyle changes, such as regular exercise, stress reduction, and adequate sleep, can also support healing on a genetic level by promoting optimal gene expression and function.

Environmental detoxification: Environmental toxins, such as heavy metals, pesticides, and pollutants, disrupt gene function and expression. Detoxification techniques support the body in eliminating these toxins and promoting optimal gene function.

Overall, epigenetic therapy is an approach to family lineage healing that recognizes the role of genetics in inherited patterns of illness or disease. Individuals promote healing on a genetic level and break free from negative patterns that may have been passed down through the family lineage by identifying and treating genetic mutations and imbalances and by supporting optimal gene expression through diet, lifestyle, and other techniques.

Conclusion

Family lineage healing techniques aim to help individuals gain insight into the inherited patterns that may impact their lives and provide them with tools to release these patterns and create a healthier, more promising future.

How Do I Know if Family Lineage Healing is for Me?

There are a few signs that indicate whether someone is a good candidate for family lineage healing:

First, you feel disconnected from your cultural heritage or family history.

Feeling disconnected from your cultural heritage or family history is a common experience for many people, especially if there has been a disconnection from traditional practices or cultural traditions over the generations. This triggers feeling lost or disconnected from one's identity, roots, and community.

This disconnection results in ancestral trauma, such as forced migration, cultural assimilation, or loss of cultural traditions due to oppression or persecution. When these experiences are not acknowledged or healed, they can be passed down through generations, resulting in disconnection from cultural heritage and a lack of understanding of one's ancestral roots.

Reconnecting with one's cultural heritage can help bring a sense of grounding, purpose, and connection to one's identity. This can involve exploring family history and learning about cultural traditions and practices, connecting with community members who share your heritage, and participating in cultural events and activities.

Additionally, seeking support from a healer, therapist or counselor specializing in intergenerational trauma and family lineage healing can be a valuable tool in the healing process. Through therapy, you can explore and process any experiences of ancestral trauma and work towards re-establishing a connection to your cultural heritage and family history.

You feel that there is something more, something huge in store for you that your soul is ready to experience.

Feeling like there is something more to explore and discover about your family lineage and sensing that your soul is ready for this journey can be a powerful indicator that family lineage healing is for you.

When we sense there is more to discover about our ancestors and family history, we are ready to explore deeper aspects of our identity and heritage. This involves researching the stories, experiences, and emotions passed down through generations and understanding their impact on our lives.

Through this process, we become more aware of ourselves and our place in the world and connect with a sense of purpose and meaning rooted in our ancestral heritage. This also aids healing from any ancestral trauma that may have been passed down and breaks inherited pain and suffering cycles.

Ultimately, engaging in family lineage healing is a transformative and life-changing experience that brings peace, connection, and growth to our lives. If you feel drawn to explore this path, it is worth seeking support from a healer, therapist, or counselor specializing in intergenerational trauma and family lineage healing.

You feel there is something that does not allow you to move forward in all areas of life.

Feeling like something is holding you back or blocking your progress in various areas of life can indicate that family lineage issues are impacting you. These blockages can manifest in multiple ways, such as recurring patterns of behavior or emotions that seem difficult to change or physical or mental health issues that persist despite attempts to address them.

These blockages may sometimes be rooted in ancestral trauma, such as past events or experiences passed down through the generations. When these experiences are not acknowledged or healed, they can continue to influence our thoughts, behaviors, and experiences, preventing us from moving forward.

By exploring your family lineage and working towards healing any ancestral trauma, you can begin to break these blockages and move forward in all areas of life. This can involve connecting with your cultural heritage and family history and seeking support from a specialized healer, therapist, or counselor specializing in intergenerational trauma and family lineage healing.

Ultimately, engaging in family lineage healing can be a powerful tool for growth and transformation, helping you release any blocks and move towards a more fulfilling life.

You see the same patterns in multiple members of your family.

Seeing similar patterns or experiences across multiple members of your family can indicate that unresolved family lineage issues are impacting the entire family system. These patterns can manifest in various ways, such as recurring relationship dynamics, health issues, emotional struggles, or behavioral patterns that seem to repeat across generations.

When these patterns are not acknowledged or addressed, they can continue to be passed down through the generations, perpetuating cycles of pain and suffering. By exploring your family lineage and working towards healing any ancestral trauma, you can begin to break these patterns and create new, healthier patterns for future generations.

Family lineage healing can involve connecting with your cultural heritage and family history and seeking support from a healer, therapist or counselor specializing in intergenerational trauma and family lineage healing. This can help you to understand the root causes of the patterns you see in your family and work towards healing and releasing them.

Ultimately, engaging in family lineage healing can bring healing and growth to you and multiple generations of your family. By breaking cycles of pain and suffering, you can create a brighter future for yourself and those you love.

You experienced personal trauma and know family members who have experienced the same.

Experiencing personal trauma and knowing other family members who have experienced similar trauma can indicate that unresolved family lineage issues impact you and your family.

Trauma can have a profound and lasting impact on our lives, and when it is not acknowledged or addressed, it can continue to be passed down through the generations. This can create cycles of pain and suffering that can persist for many years and affect multiple generations of a family.

Through family lineage healing, you can explore the experiences and emotions passed down through your family and work towards healing any ancestral trauma that may be contributing to your struggles. This can involve connecting with your cultural heritage and family history and seeking support from a healer, therapist or counselor specializing in intergenerational trauma and family lineage healing.

By acknowledging and healing the ancestral trauma that may impact you and your family, you can break these cycles of pain and suffering and create a brighter future for yourself and those you love. This can bring peace, healing, and growth to your life, helping you move forward and create a promising, more gratifying future.

You have been abused physically, sexually, verbally, and psychologically.

Experiencing abuse can indicate that unresolved family lineage issues impact you and your family. When abuse is not acknowledged or addressed, it can continue to be passed down through the generations, perpetuating cycles of pain and suffering.

Through family lineage healing, you can explore the experiences and emotions passed down through your family and work towards healing any ancestral trauma contributing to your struggles.

It's important to note that healing from abuse is a process that can take time and can be difficult. Still, with the proper support, it can be an incredibly empowering and transformative experience.

It's vital to seek support from a trained healer, therapist or counselor who can help you work through your experiences and emotions and help you to develop coping skills and strategies for moving forward in a healthy and fulfilling way. It can be essential to restore balance and harmony within the bloodline.

You have extreme emotions: fear, sadness, anger, forgiveness issues, resentment, or suffer from anxiety, depression, constant doubt, confusion, or chronic pain.

Experiencing extreme emotions, anxiety, fear, depression, chronic pain, and other psychological, spiritual, or physical symptoms can be signs of unresolved family lineage issues impacting you and your family.

Inherited trauma and emotions can be passed down from generation to generation, perpetuating cycles of pain and suffering. When this trauma and emotional baggage is not acknowledged or addressed, it can contribute to various psychological, spiritual, and physical symptoms, including those mentioned above.

Through family lineage healing, you can explore the experiences and emotions passed down through your family and work towards healing any ancestral trauma contributing to your struggles. This can involve connecting with your cultural heritage and family history and seeking support from a professional healer, therapist, or counselors specializing in intergenerational trauma and family lineage healing.

By acknowledging and healing the ancestral trauma that may impact you and your family, you can break these cycles of pain and suffering and create a more positive, and healthier future for yourself and those you love. This can help to reduce symptoms of anxiety, depression, and chronic pain and bring a sense of peace, healing, and growth to your life.

It's important to remember that healing is a process that can take time and can be difficult. Still, with the proper support, it can be an incredibly empowering and transformative experience. For example, suppose you are struggling with extreme emotions, chronic pain, or other psychological symptoms. In that case, seeking support from a qualified spiritual healer, therapist, or counselor who can help guide you through the healing process is essential.

You have a health challenge for which you cannot find a solution, or doctors have been unable to resolve it.

Experiencing a health challenge that you cannot find a solution to or that doctors have not been able to resolve may be a sign of an underlying issue in your family lineage that needs to be addressed. Family lineage healing can help you identify and heal these unresolved issues to experience more excellent health, well-being, and connection to your ancestry.

It can also help explore your family's history and identify patterns of behavior, beliefs, and emotions passed down through generations. This can include exploring family secrets, traumas, or unresolved issues that may impact your health and well-being.

Sometimes, health challenges may result from these unresolved issues passed down through your family's lineage. By addressing and healing these issues, you may find relief from your health challenges and experience greater overall well-being.

Exposure to family lineage healing can also connect you to your family history and ancestry. In addition, by understanding the experiences and struggles of your ancestors, you may gain insight into your own life and find healing to your health challenges.

Family lineage healing can be a powerful tool for improving your health and well-being and connecting with your family history and heritage. If you are struggling with a health challenge you cannot resolve, it may be worth exploring this approach to see if it can provide the healing and insight you need.

Note

Suppose you are experiencing any of these signs. In that case, seeking support through healing and counseling may be helpful. You can explore your experiences and emotions through therapy and work towards healing and growth. Connecting with your cultural heritage and learning about traditional healing practices can also be valuable to the healing journey.

Does Family Lineage Healing Belong to a Belief System?

Family lineage healing practice is not tied to specific religious or spiritual traditions. However, it may draw upon various spiritual or cultural practices emphasizing the importance of ancestral connection and healing.

The practice of family lineage healing often involves a deep exploration of one's family history, including examining patterns of illness, addiction, or trauma that may have been passed down through the generations. This process can be emotionally challenging, as it may bring up painful memories or unresolved issues from the past. However, family lineage healing aims to bring these issues to light to promote healing and growth.

Family lineage healing can be approached from various perspectives, including psychotherapy, energy healing, ancestral clearing, and other modalities. Regardless of the specific approach, the goal is to identify and address the root causes of inherited patterns of illness or dysfunction to break the cycle and promote healing on a deep level.

Family lineage healing can be a profoundly spiritual practice but is not necessarily tied to any specific religious tradition or belief system. Instead, it draws upon collective spiritual values, morals, ethics, and practices common to many cultures and traditions.

These values and practices emphasize the interconnectedness of all living beings and the importance of honoring and respecting one's ancestors and the legacy that they have passed down. This recognition of the impact of the past on the present is a central tenet of family lineage healing.

The healing in family lineage is not limited to the conscious mind. Still, it extends to the subconscious mind, soul, and the imprinted mental and emotional energy patterns all humans carry. Therefore, recognizing the importance of energy patterns is crucial to many spiritual and energetic practices and an essential element of family lineage healing.

While family lineage healing may draw upon various spiritual or cultural practices, it does not create conflict or contradict any religious belief. Instead, it can be adapted to align with a wide range of spiritual or religious convictions, as it is focused on healing and growth on a deep level that transcends any particular religious or cultural framework.

Overall, family lineage healing is a powerful approach that recognizes the interrelation of all living beings and the importance of honoring one's ancestors and the legacy they have passed down. While it is rooted in collective spiritual values and practices, it is not tied to any identifiable religious or cultural tradition. Instead, it can be adapted to meet the needs of individuals from all backgrounds and belief systems.

Emotional Healing

Emotional healing addresses and resolves emotional pain, familial conflicts, trauma, and unresolved emotions passed down from previous generations that may affect an individual's mental, emotional, and physical well-being. Family lineage healing recognizes that families can often carry emotional wounds and trauma for generations without realizing it. These wounds can manifest in various ways, such as in patterns of negative thinking, unhealthy coping mechanisms, and self-destructive behavior. Emotional healing then involves exploring and processing these emotions and experiences, often with the guidance of a therapist or other mental health professional.

Emotional healing aims to help individuals break free from these patterns by examining the root causes of emotional pain. It, in turn, allows them to create a healthier and more positive future by developing greater self-awareness, self-compassion, and self-love. This process may involve various methods such as talk therapy, cognitive-behavioral therapy, meditation, mindfulness, and somatic therapy. Emotional healing can help individuals break free from patterns of behavior and experiences that have been holding them back and lead to improved relationships with themselves and others, increased resilience, and a greater sense of well-being.

Impact of Emotional Healing in Family Lineage Healing

Emotional healing plays a crucial role in understanding and addressing patterns of behavior and experiences passed down through generations. This is because unprocessed emotions and trauma can continue to affect individuals and their family members long after the initial event.

Exploring family history and behavior patterns is important to identify unresolved emotions and trauma. This may involve examining family stories, conflicts, and relationships, as well as exploring one's own emotions and experiences. It may also be helpful to seek the support of a therapist or other mental health professional trained in trauma and family systems work.

Once unresolved emotions and trauma have been identified, processing them is essential to emotional healing. This may involve techniques such as spiritual healing, meditation, mindfulness, or journaling to help individuals become more aware of their thoughts and feelings. It may also involve more structured forms of therapy, such as cognitive-behavioral or trauma-focused therapy, which can help individuals process and work through difficult emotions and experiences.

In addition to individual healing, addressing unresolved emotions and trauma within the more extensive family system may be necessary. This may involve family therapy or other group therapy to help family members understand and address behavior patterns passed down through generations.

Overall, emotional healing is a critical component of family lineage healing. It helps individuals and families break free from patterns of behavior and experiences that may have held them back for generations. As a result, individuals can create a healthier and more positive future for themselves and their families by identifying and processing unresolved emotions and trauma.

Spiritual Connection

Spiritual connection in family lineage healing refers to the belief that there is a spiritual dimension to the intergenerational patterns and traumas that can affect families across generations. According to this perspective, these patterns and traumas can be passed down through the family lineage. They can manifest in different ways, such as physical, spiritual, or emotional symptoms, behavior patterns, or relationship dynamics.

Spiritual connection in family lineage healing involves recognizing and acknowledging these intergenerational patterns and traumas and working to heal them through a combination of spiritual and therapeutic practices. This can include meditation, prayer, energy healing, and connecting with ancestral spirits or guides.

By spiritually healing these intergenerational patterns and traumas, individuals and families break free from negative patterns and move towards a more harmonious and fulfilling way of being. This involves a deeper connection to one's family history and ancestral lineage and a sense of purpose or meaning that comes from understanding and embracing one's roots.

The Role of Spirituality in Family Lineage Healing

Spirituality plays a vital role in family lineage healing by providing a deeper connection to one's ancestry and a greater sense of purpose and meaning in life. Here are some ways in which spirituality contributes to family lineage healing:

Connecting with ancestors: Many spiritual practices involve honoring and connecting with ancestors. This includes rituals, prayers, or simply setting aside time to reflect on and remember one's ancestors. Connecting with one's ancestors allows individuals to deeply understand their family history and the challenges and triumphs that their ancestors faced. This provides a sense of continuity and connection to one's past.

Understanding family patterns: Through spiritual practices such as meditation, introspection, and reflection, individuals learn about the patterns passed down through their family lineage. This includes patterns of behavior, relationships, or even health issues. By becoming aware of these patterns, individuals break negative cycles and create healthier patterns for themselves and future generations.

Finding meaning and purpose: Spirituality also presents a greater meaning and purpose in life. Individuals feel more grounded and fulfilled by connecting with a higher power or a greater sense of purpose. This provides direction and motivation for healing family patterns and creates a positive legacy for future generations.

Practicing forgiveness: Forgiveness is a core aspect of family lineage healing. Through spiritual practices such as prayer, meditation, or forgiveness rituals, individuals work on releasing past hurts and resentments. This produces a more positive and loving environment within the family, leading to greater harmony and connection between family members.

Finally, spirituality provides a powerful tool for healing family lineage patterns. By connecting with ancestors, understanding family patterns, finding meaning and purpose, and practicing forgiveness, individuals can create a positive legacy for future generations and foster greater harmony and connection within their families.

Physical Health and Well-being

Family lineage healing involves exploring and understanding the family history and identifying and releasing any negative patterns or energies that may affect the current generation. The negative patterns or energies may affect the Physical health and well-being of an individual or group of people.

Physical health and well-being are important aspects of family lineage healing. Inherited patterns and traumas manifest in the body as physical ailments, so addressing and healing these underlying issues positively impact physical health.

For example, suppose a heart disease or high blood pressure pattern in a family lineage. In that case, exploring the emotional and psychological factors contributing to these physical conditions may be beneficial. By understanding and releasing any negative emotions or limiting beliefs related to these conditions, individuals can work towards improving their physical health and preventing future generations from inheriting these patterns.

Similarly, exploring and releasing any inherited traumas or negative patterns related to substance abuse or addiction allow individuals to break free from these cycles and improve their physical health and well-being.

In addition to addressing inherited patterns and traumas, family lineage healing promotes positive health practices and behaviors within a family. This includes encouraging healthy eating habits, regular exercise, stress management techniques, and other self-care practices that support physical health and well-being.

By working towards healing and releasing negative patterns and energies within a family lineage, individuals support their health and the health of future generations.

Impact of Inherited Patterns of Illness on Physical Health

Inherited patterns of illness can have a significant impact on physical health. Inherited patterns refer to the transmission of genetic and epigenetic factors that increase the risk of developing certain health conditions. They also indicate the transmission of non-genetic factors such as lifestyle behaviors, environmental exposures, and cultural beliefs that increase the risk of developing certain health conditions.

The impact of inherited patterns on physical health varies depending on the specific condition or pattern and individual factors such as age, gender, and lifestyle choices.

However, some common ways that inherited patterns impact physical health include the following:

Increased risk of certain health conditions: Certain genetic and epigenetic factors increase the risk of developing specific health conditions, such as cardiovascular disease, cancer, and diabetes. Inherited lifestyle behaviors, such as unhealthy diet and lack of physical activity, also intensify the risk of developing these conditions.

Earlier onset of health conditions: Inherited patterns also increase the likelihood of developing health conditions at an earlier age than is typical. For example, some genetic factors may heighten the risk of developing certain types of cancer at a younger age than is typically seen.

Greater severity of health conditions: Inherited patterns also influence the severity of health conditions. For example, some genetic factors may increase the severity of symptoms of certain health conditions, such as asthma or autoimmune disorders.

Increased vulnerability to environmental exposures: Inherited patterns also impact how individuals respond to environmental exposures, such as exposure to toxins or pollutants. Several genetic factors may reinforce the vulnerability of specific individuals to these exposures, leading to a greater risk of developing associated health conditions.

Psychological impact: Inherited patterns of illness also affect individuals psychologically, leading to feelings of anxiety, stress, and fear related to their risk of developing certain health conditions.

Overall, inherited patterns of illness significantly impact physical health by increasing the risk of certain health conditions and affecting the severity of symptoms. However, it is essential to note that inherited patterns are not the sole determinant of an individual's health, and lifestyle factors such as healthy eating habits, regular exercise, and stress management also play a significant role in preventing and managing inherited patterns of illness.

How Family Lineage Healing Can Improve Overall Physical Health and Well-being.

Family lineage healing can positively impact overall physical health and well-being. Here are a few examples:

Addressing inherited patterns and traumas: Family lineage healing involves exploring and understanding the family history and identifying any negative patterns or traumas passed down through generations. By managing and healing these underlying issues, individuals will release any emotional and psychological blockages contributing to physical health issues.

Reducing stress and anxiety: Inherited patterns of stress and anxiety can manifest in physical symptoms such as headaches, high blood pressure, and digestive issues. Addressing and releasing inherited stress and anxiety patterns help individuals reduce their risk of developing these physical symptoms.

Encouraging healthy lifestyle behaviors: Family lineage healing also involves promoting positive health practices and behaviors within a family. This may include encouraging healthy eating habits, regular exercise, stress management techniques, and other self-care practices that support physical health and well-being.

Improving communication and relationships: Family lineage healing enables individuals to improve their relationships with family members and to develop healthier communication patterns. This reduces stress and improves overall emotional well-being, which in turn can have a positive impact on physical health.

Enhancing self-awareness: Family lineage healing helps individuals better understand themselves and their family history. This enhanced self-awareness allows individuals to make more informed choices about their health and well-being and to make changes that can support their overall physical health.

Practical Strategies for Integrating Family Lineage Healing into Your Daily Life

Integrating family lineage healing into daily life is a powerful way to connect with and honor your ancestors and to heal any intergenerational wounds affecting your life.

This includes a range of strategies depending on your individual needs and preferences. Here are some practical strategies that you may find helpful, depending on your cultural, religious, or spiritual beliefs:

Create a family altar.

Creating an altar is not to worship your ancestors. It is to connect and honor them as the ones who came before you and the roots of the trees producing the branches you are part of. That altar is a sacred space where you can sit quietly to be in the energy of your ancestors. Setting up a unique space in your home to honor your ancestors can be a powerful way to integrate family lineage healing into your daily life. For example, you could place photos of your ancestors, items that belonged to them, or other meaningful objects on the altar and take a few moments each day to reflect on their legacy. Creating a family altar can deepen your connection to your ancestors and cultivate a daily practice of reflection and gratitude.

Here are some additional insights and tips for setting up your family altar:

Choose a location: Select a place in your home that feels meaningful and special. This could be a corner of your bedroom, a shelf in your living room, or any other location that feels right.

Decide on a theme: Consider the theme or intention of your altar. This could be to honor your ancestors, to connect with your spiritual or religious beliefs, or to celebrate a particular aspect of your heritage or culture.

Select meaningful items: Choose items to place on the altar that has personal significance to you and your family. This could include photos of your ancestors, things that belonged to them, candles, crystals, flowers, or any other items with special meaning.

Set the mood: Create a calming and reflective atmosphere around your altar by incorporating soft lighting, calming scents, or other elements that help you feel centered and connected.

Make it a daily practice: Take a few moments each day to reflect on your altar and connect with your ancestors. For example, you could light a candle or incense, say a prayer, or sit quietly and reflect on their legacy and how they have influenced your life.

Remember that your family altar is a personal and sacred space; feel free to customize it meaningfully and authentically. Creating a family altar deepens your connection to your ancestors and helps you cultivate a daily practice of reflection and gratitude.

Engage in regular meditation or energy healing practices.

Meditation and energy healing practices are powerful tools for connecting with your ancestors and healing intergenerational wounds. You could set aside a few minutes daily to meditate, receive spiritual healing or engage in other energy-healing practices that resonate with you.

Here are some additional insights and tips for incorporating these practices into your daily routine:

Start small: If you're new to meditation, Sufi spiritual healing, or energy healing practices, it is important to start small and work your way up. Begin with just a few minutes each day and gradually increase the time as you become more comfortable with the practice.

Find a style that works for you: There are many different types of meditation and energy healing practices, so it is important to find a style that resonates with you. For example, you might try guided meditations, breathwork, sound healing or Sufi spiritual healing, or other energy healing practices to see what feels most effective, in the highest light, and more beneficial for you. These practices can also help reduce stress, increase inner peace and clarity, and cultivate a deeper spiritual connection.

Be consistent: Consistency is vital in meditation and energy healing practices. Set aside a regular time each day to practice and make it a non-negotiable part of your daily routine.

Visualization can be essential for connecting with your ancestors and healing intergenerational wounds. As you meditate or engage in energy healing practices, visualize yourself connecting with your ancestors and releasing any negative energy or patterns passed down through the generations.

Consider working with a practitioner: If you're struggling to connect with your ancestors or heal intergenerational wounds, consider working with a healer, therapist or practitioner specializing in these areas. They can provide guidance, support, and personalized tools to help you navigate the process.

Develop a self-care plan.
Developing a self-care plan is an integral part of family lineage healing. Caring for your own physical, emotional, and spiritual well-being will create a foundation of strength and resilience to help you navigate any challenges in your healing journey. Consider developing a self-care plan that includes exercise, healthy eating, time in nature, and activities that bring you joy.

Some additional insights and tips for developing a self-care plan:
Start with the basics: Developing a self-care plan does not have to be complicated. Start by focusing on the basics, such as getting enough sleep, eating a healthy diet, and exercising regularly.
Identify activities that bring joy: Self-care is more than taking care of your physical health. Identifying actions that bring you joy and make you feel fulfilled is also important. This could be anything from reading a good book to spending time in nature to taking a relaxing bath.
Make time for spiritual practices: Connecting with your spirituality can be an important part of family lineage healing. Consider incorporating regular meditation, prayer, or other spiritual practices into your self-care plan.

Practice self-compassion: It is essential to approach your self-care plan with compassion and kindness. Remember that self-care is not about being perfect but about doing the best you can to take care of yourself at the moment.

Make it a priority: Finally, make your self-care plan a priority. Set aside dedicated time each day or each week to engage in activities that support your physical, emotional, and spiritual well-being.

Developing a self-care plan creates a strong foundation for your family lineage healing journey. Taking care of yourself in these ways can help to reduce stress, increase resilience, and cultivate a greater sense of inner peace and well-being.

Seek professional support.

Healing intergenerational wounds involves addressing and working through the emotional, psychological, and sometimes physical trauma passed down from one generation to the next. This trauma can manifest in various ways, including behavior patterns, negative beliefs, and chronic emotional pain. In addition, these wounds can be passed down through families and communities and profoundly impact an individual's mental and physical well-being.

Working with a therapist or other healing professional specializing in intergenerational healing offers many benefits. These professionals are trained to help individuals identify patterns and beliefs rooted in past trauma and support them in healing. In addition, they may use a variety of modalities, including talk therapy, somatic therapy, and trauma-informed yoga, to help individuals process their emotions and find healing.

Additionally, healing professionals provide a safe and supportive space for individuals to explore and address their intergenerational wounds. This is particularly important for individuals who may not have felt comfortable or safe discussing their family history or trauma with others.

Finding a therapist or healing professional with experience and training in intergenerational healing is helpful when seeking professional support. You may want to ask potential therapists or professionals about their experience working with intergenerational trauma and what approaches they use to support healing. Finding a therapist or professional you feel comfortable working with and whom you feel understands your unique needs and experiences can also be helpful.

Overall, seeking out professional support is an essential step in the process of healing intergenerational wounds. With the guidance and support of a trained professional, individuals can find healing and move towards a more positive and fulfilling future.

Research your family history.

Researching your family history and genealogy can be a rich and rewarding experience that can provide a deeper understanding of your family's past and help you connect with your ancestors. Learning about your family's story can also provide insight into the patterns, beliefs, and wounds passed down through the generations, which can be a valuable first step toward healing intergenerational wounds.

There are many resources available for conducting family history research. Online resources such as ancestry.com and familysearch.org offer access to a wealth of historical records, including census records, military records, and birth and death certificates. Local archives and historical societies can also be excellent resources, as they may have records and documents unavailable online.

In addition to conducting research online and in archives, talking to family members can be an important way to learn about your family history. Older family members may have stories and information not available in historical records, and they may be able to provide a more personal perspective on your family's past. Recording these conversations can also be a valuable way to preserve your family's story for future generations.

As you conduct your research, it can be helpful to keep a record of the information you uncover, such as birth and death dates, immigration records, and stories or anecdotes about your ancestors. This information can be organized into a family tree or genealogy chart, visually representing your family's history.

Note

By integrating these strategies into your daily life, you can begin to honor your ancestors and heal any intergenerational wounds that may be affecting your life.

Common Obstacles to Family Lineage Healing

Healing intergenerational wounds and exploring one's family lineage can be a complex and emotional journey that is not without its obstacles. The most common barriers to family lineage healing include resistance from family members, lack of information about one's ancestry, and difficulty processing unresolved emotions. Here's more about each of these obstacles:

Resistance from family members

One of the most common obstacles to exploring one's family lineage is resistance from family members. Family members may be uncomfortable discussing past traumas or may not want to revisit painful memories. Sometimes, family members may actively resist attempts to uncover the family history and lineage. This resistance can make it difficult to discover information and may require sensitivity and patience when engaging with family members.

Lack of information about one's ancestry

Another common obstacle to family lineage healing is a need for more information about one's ancestry. This can be due to lost or destroyed records, lack of family documentation, or limited access to historical records. In some cases, it may be necessary to conduct extensive research to uncover information about one's ancestry.

Difficulty processing unresolved emotions

Difficulty processing unresolved emotions can be an obstacle to family lineage healing. This can be especially difficult for individuals who have experienced intergenerational trauma or abuse. Therefore, it is essential to approach the healing process with self-compassion and seek support from trained professionals.

Exploring one's family lineage and healing intergenerational wounds can be challenging but rewarding. By understanding common obstacles and seeking support from trained professionals and loved ones, individuals can navigate them and move towards more incredible healing and understanding of their family's history.

How is the Healing Process Done?

The process of healing lineage or ancestral patterns is an experiential one that can involve various techniques and practices to help create a deeper connection with the soul and facilitate the release of limiting beliefs or patterns passed down through generations. These techniques can include guided practices, advanced imagery, movements, breathwork, and sound healing.

Guided meditation or visualization exercises can be powerful tools in healing lineage or ancestral patterns. These practices can help individuals access more profound levels of consciousness and connect spiritually with their ancestral lineage.

Meditation

In the context of healing lineage or ancestral patterns, meditation can be a powerful tool for accessing more profound levels of the subconscious mind and promoting a sense of connection with our ancestors.

Through meditation, we can quiet the mind and bring our attention inward, allowing us to access deeper levels of our consciousness. We can release stored emotional blocks or trauma affecting our present lives by focusing our awareness on our breath, bodily sensations, or a particular object or visualization.

Meditation can also help us to connect with our ancestors on a spiritual level. By quieting the mind and creating a receptive state, we can open ourselves up to messages or insights from our ancestors or cultivate a deeper sense of connection and belonging to our lineage.

Some meditation practices may also focus on specific intentions or affirmations related to healing our ancestral patterns. For example, we may repeat affirmations such as "I release the limiting beliefs and patterns of my ancestors" or "I am free to create my path in life." Repeating these affirmations can shift our subconscious beliefs and create a path toward more incredible healing and transformation.

Visualization

Visualization exercises involve using the power of imagination to create mental images or scenarios that promote healing and transformation. They can be a powerful tool for accessing subconscious beliefs or patterns, connecting with our ancestral lineage, and releasing emotional blocks or stored trauma from the body.

Visualization exercises involve using the power of imagination to create mental images or scenarios that promote healing and transformation. These exercises can help us access the subconscious mind, where our beliefs and patterns are stored. By using visualization techniques, we can bring these beliefs and patterns to our conscious awareness and begin to release them.

In the context of healing lineage or ancestral patterns, visualization exercises can be used to connect with our ancestral lineage on a spiritual level. For example, we may visualize ourselves standing at the center of a circle of ancestors or walking down a path with our ancestors guiding us. By creating these mental images, we can cultivate a more profound sense of connection and belonging to our lineage.

Visualization exercises can also release emotional blocks or stored trauma from the body. For example, we may visualize a symbol or object representing our emotional block or trauma and then imagine it gradually dissolving or being released from our bodies. By creating these mental images, we can release stored emotions and trauma from the body and build a sense of inner calm and peace.

Overall, a practitioner or teacher can guide both meditation and visualization exercises. They help to create a safe and supportive environment and provide instructions and prompts to facilitate the process. By accessing more profound levels of the subconscious and promoting a sense of connection with our lineage, these practices can help to release limiting beliefs and patterns and create a path towards greater healing and transformation.

Advanced Imagery

Advanced imagery techniques can be a powerful tool for uncovering subconscious beliefs or patterns affecting an individual's life. These techniques involve using the power of imagination to explore deep subconscious levels and bring hidden patterns or beliefs to light.

One example of an advanced imagery technique is regression; used by psychotherapists. This technique involves guiding an individual into a deeply relaxed state and then using imagery to explore past experiences or memories affecting their current life. By accessing these past experiences, the individual can gain insight into the subconscious beliefs or patterns formed and begin to release them.

Another example of an advanced imagery technique is archetypal imagery. This technique explores the archetypes or universal symbols in the individual's subconscious. By using visualization and other techniques, the individual can begin to uncover the archetypes that are most active in their subconscious and gain insight into the patterns or beliefs that these archetypes represent.

Using the power of imagination to explore deep levels of the subconscious, we can bring hidden patterns or beliefs to light, gain insight into their origins, and begin to release them. This can lead to a greater sense of inner peace and well-being and help individuals to overcome obstacles or challenges that may have been holding them back.

Movement

Movements can be used to release emotional blocks and stored trauma from the body. Emotions and trauma can become stuck in the body, creating physical sensations and pain. By using movements and other physical practices, we can help to release these blocks and promote healing on a deep level.

One example of a movement-based practice that can be used in family lineage healing is yoga. Yoga involves a series of postures or asanas designed to stretch and strengthen the body while promoting relaxation and inner peace. By practicing yoga, individuals can release tension and stress from their bodies and open up energy channels that may have been blocked.

Another example of a movement-based practice is dance. Dance is a powerful tool for releasing emotion and trauma from the body, as it involves using the body to express and release pent-up energy. By moving the body naturally and expressively, individuals can release stored emotion and promote healing on a deep level.

Other movement-based practices that can be used in family lineage healing includes trauma release exercises (TRE), yoga, tai chi, qigong, and other forms of martial arts. These practices involve slow, deliberate movements designed to promote relaxation, inner peace, and a greater sense of connection with the body and the world around us.

Overall, movements can be a powerful tool for releasing emotional blocks and stored trauma from the body. By using the body to express and release pent-up energy, we can promote healing on a deep level and move towards a greater sense of inner peace and well-being.

Sound Healing

Sound healing can also be a powerful tool in healing lineage or ancestral patterns. Specific frequencies or vibrations can help clear energetic blockages and promote healing on a physical, emotional, and spiritual level. In addition, using sacred sound or chants with divine attributes can help create a sense of safety and support, which can be particularly important when working with deep-seated emotions or trauma.

Sound healing can take many forms, but some practices involve the use of chants and vibration frequency transmitted from dhikr with Divine Attributes or Sufi sound healing instruments, Tibetan singing bowls, gongs, drums, or tuning forks. These instruments produce a range of frequencies and vibrations that can be felt throughout the body, helping to clear energetic blockages and promote a sense of relaxation and well-being.

For example, the sound of a singing bowl may produce a deep, resonant vibration that can help soothe the nervous system and promote relaxation. Tuning forks may involve applying specific frequencies to acupressure points or areas of the body to promote healing and balance. The sound of a gong may produce a wide range of frequencies and overtones that can help to clear stagnant energy and promote a sense of release.

Sound healing can be potent in healing lineage or ancestral patterns. This is because certain frequencies or vibrations may be associated with specific emotions or states of being. Therefore, by using these frequencies in a targeted way, it may be possible to release stored trauma or emotions related to our ancestral lineage.

For example, 528 Hz is often associated with healing and transformation, while 417 Hz is associated with clearing negative energy and promoting change. Using sound healing techniques that incorporate these frequencies makes it possible to release old patterns and beliefs holding us back from living fully in the present.

Overall, using sound healing in the context of family lineage healing can be a powerful tool for promoting healing and transformation. By creating a sense of safety and support and using targeted frequencies and vibrations to clear energetic blockages, individuals can connect more deeply with their ancestral lineage and release limiting beliefs or patterns that may be holding them back from living a fulfilling and empowered life.

Ritual and Ceremony

Rituals and ceremonies can be important components in healing lineage or ancestral patterns. These practices can help create a sacred and safe space for the individual and provide a sense of connection to their ancestors and spiritual guides. **Here are some examples of how these practices can be used:**

Lighting candles: Candles can be lit to symbolize a connection to the individual's ancestors or to represent a particular intention or prayer. For example, a candle can be burned to honor a specific ancestor or to symbolize the release of a particular emotion or belief that no longer serves the individual.

Burning incense, sage, or asafoetida resin (enemy of the devil): The burning of incense, sage, or asafoetida resin can clear the energy of a space and create a sense of ritual. This practice can help the individual to connect with their ancestral lineage and to develop an understanding of focus during the healing process.

Offering prayers: Prayers can be delivered to ancestors or spiritual guides, asking for guidance or support in healing. These prayers can be spoken, written, and placed on an altar or other sacred space.

Creating an altar or sacred space: An altar or sacred space can represent the individual's connection to their ancestors and hold objects or symbols that are meaningful to them.

In summary, rituals and ceremonies can be used in various ways to support the healing process of lineage or ancestral patterns. These practices can help create a sense of intention and focus and provide a sense of connection to the individual's ancestors and spiritual guides.

Integration

Integrating the healing work into daily life is essential to healing lineage or ancestral patterns. This can involve creating new habits or practices that support a sense of connection and balance, such as daily meditation or mindfulness exercises, journaling, or spending time in nature.

Here are some examples of how different practices can be integrated into everyday life:

Daily meditation or mindfulness exercises: Heart-based meditation or mindfulness activities can be incorporated into everyday life as a regular practice. This can involve setting aside a specific time for meditation or self-reflection each day, such as first thing in the morning or before bed. Even just a few minutes of meditation or mindfulness can significantly reduce stress and promote a sense of calm and focus. (Heart-based meditation or exercises are commonly used to open and witness the state of the heart, calm the mind and cultivate self-awareness. In addition, regular practice allows individuals to observe their thoughts and feelings without judgment and develop a greater sense of presence and peace. This can be particularly helpful for those seeking to heal lineage or ancestral patterns, as it can help to create a sense of inner space and detachment from difficult emotions or thought patterns.

Many forms of meditation and self-reflection practices include heart centered, breath awareness, body scanning, visualization, and loving-kindness practices. It can be helpful to experiment with different techniques to find the ones that resonate most with an individual's needs and preferences. For example, some people may find incorporating a guided meditation or self-reflection practice through a teacher or an app beneficial. In contrast, others may prefer to practice on their own.

Incorporating meditation or self-reflection practices into daily life can also help to establish a greater sense of routine and structure, which can be important for those seeking to create a new sense of balance or connection with their ancestry. By making meditation or self-reflection a regular part of daily life, individuals can establish a consistent and reliable source of support, regardless of external circumstances or challenges that may arise.

Journaling: Journaling is a valuable tool for personal growth and self-awareness. Regularly writing down thoughts and emotions can help individuals identify patterns and beliefs that may hold them back. It can also be a way to process difficult emotions, gain perspective on a situation, and develop a deeper understanding of oneself.

Regular journaling can also help individuals to track their progress as they work on healing lineage or ancestral patterns. By recording insights, breakthroughs, and challenges, they can see how far they have come and what areas they still need to work on. This can be a valuable source of motivation and encouragement on their healing journey.

Journaling can take many forms, from free writing to more structured prompts or exercises. It can also be combined with other healing practices, such as meditation or visualization. For example, an individual may start their journaling session with a few minutes of meditation to help them connect with their inner wisdom and intuition. They may then use journaling prompts to explore a particular issue or challenge or reflect on their progress in their healing journey.

The act of writing itself can also be therapeutic. Putting pen to paper can help to release pent-up emotions, express oneself more freely, and gain a deeper understanding of one's thoughts and feelings. By making journaling a regular part of their daily routine, individuals can create a space for self-reflection and growth and cultivate a deeper connection with themselves and their inner wisdom.

Spending time in nature: Spending time in nature has been shown to have numerous physical, emotional, and spiritual benefits. Nature has a way of soothing and calming the mind and body, reducing stress, and promoting relaxation. In addition, research has found that spending time in nature can lower blood pressure, reduce muscle tension, and boost the immune system.

Regarding emotional and spiritual benefits, spending time in nature can help foster a sense of connection with the world. This can be particularly important for individuals working to heal ancestral patterns. It can help them feel a sense of belonging and connectedness to their ancestors and the natural world.

One way to incorporate nature into daily life is to take a daily walk in the nearby park or natural area, practice yoga or other mindful movements outside, or take a few deep breaths to connect with the natural environment. This can be a chance to unplug technology, breathe fresh air, and connect with the natural world. Exercising regularly or practicing other mindful movements outdoors can also be a powerful way to connect with nature and the body.

Simply taking a few deep breaths outside can be a way to connect with the heart and natural environment. One can close their eyes, take a few deep breaths, and imagine breathing in the energy of the natural world. This can be a simple and effective way to incorporate nature into daily life and promote a sense of connection and balance.

Note

The healing process can be experiential and involve various techniques, such as guided practices, imagery, movements, and sound healing. By identifying and releasing limiting beliefs or patterns that stem from our bloodlines, we can free ourselves from their influence and reclaim our power.

It's also interesting to note that healing lineage or ancestry wounds often involves connecting with the original ancestor associated with the root cause of the patterns, stories, trauma, or pain. By releasing these memories at a cellular level and reconnecting with the soul's essence, we can promote healing and create a stronger connection with our spiritual guide and divine nature.

Overall, it's essential to approach the healing process with an open mind and a willingness to explore and release the patterns that may be holding us back. Then, with the proper guidance and techniques, we can create a path toward more remarkable healing, growth, and connection with our true selves.

Who Are in Our Lineage?

Our ancestors are not just the people who came before us but the foundation upon which our lives and identities are built. They represent our family tree, stretching back through the generations, and include parents, grandparents, great-grandparents, and so on, all the way up to our distant ancestors who lived hundreds or even thousands of years ago. Each individual has a unique story; their experiences and perspectives have shaped our lives.

When we think of our ancestors, we often focus on the immediate family members we knew or heard stories about. However, our family tree is much broader and more complex than that. Beyond our parents and grandparents, there are great-grandparents, great-great-grandparents, and so on, extending back for generations. Each of these individuals played a role in shaping the genetic makeup of our family line, and many of them also directly impacted the lives of their descendants.

One of many ways our ancestors can influence us is through genetic or cellular memory. This suggests that our ancestors' experiences and traumas can be passed down through our DNA, affecting our health and behavior. While this idea is still somewhat controversial, some evidence supports it. For example, studies have shown that the children and grandchildren of Holocaust survivors are more likely to suffer from conditions such as anger or rage, anxiety, depression, and addictive patterns even if they did not experience the trauma directly.

However, even beyond genetics, our ancestors can leave a lasting impact on our lives. They may have passed down cultural traditions or values that continue to shape our identity, even if we do not always recognize it. For example, if your family has a strong tradition of religious faith, this may have been instilled in you from an early age, even if you do not practice that faith yourself. Similarly, if your ancestors were immigrants or members of a minority group, their experiences may have influenced how you view the world and your place in it.

One of the most powerful ways our ancestors can influence us is through the stories passed down through the generations. Whether these stories are told around the dinner table, recorded in family histories, or shared through oral traditions, they help us connect to our past and understand where we come from. Through these stories, we can learn about the struggles and triumphs of our ancestors and gain a deeper appreciation for their sacrifices to provide a better life for their descendants.

At the same time, however, it is important to recognize that our ancestors were human beings, just like us. They had flaws and made mistakes, and not all of their actions or beliefs may be ones that we would want to emulate. Therefore, taking a critical and nuanced approach to understanding our family history is important, acknowledging both the positive and negative aspects of our ancestors' legacies.

Ultimately, our ancestors are integral to who we are, and their impact can be felt countlessly throughout our lives.

Whether genetic memory, cultural traditions, or the stories passed down through the generations, they are a vital part of our family tree and a crucial link to our past. By embracing and understanding our ancestors, we can better appreciate our place in the world and the legacy we pass down to future generations.

The Influence of Those in Our Lineage on Us

Our family lineage can profoundly influence who we are as individuals. The people who came before us, from our parents and grandparents to our distant ancestors, all shape our identities and experiences. Here are some of the ways in which our family lineage can influence us:

Genetics: Our family lineage plays a crucial role in shaping who we are, and one of the most significant ways in which it can affect us is through genetics. Our genetic makeup is determined by the combination of genes inherited from our parents and ancestors. These genes carry instructions for everything from our physical appearance to our susceptibility to specific health conditions. As a result, our family lineage can shape a wide range of traits and characteristics that make us unique individuals.

One of the most obvious ways genetics can be passed down through our family lineage is in physical traits. For example, our genes significantly determine our physical appearance, including traits such as eye color, hair color, and height. We may also inherit other physical characteristics, such as facial features, body shape, or how we move or carry ourselves. These physical traits can be passed down through multiple generations, giving us a tangible connection to our family lineage.

In addition to physical traits, our family lineage can also influence our personality traits through genetics. While the extent to which personality traits are influenced by genetics is still a subject of debate, there is evidence to suggest that some characteristics, such as introversion or extroversion, may be at least partially heritable. This means that we may share certain personality traits with our family members. For example, we may have a similar sense of humor or share a love of the outdoors with our parents, grandparents, or siblings.

Another way our family lineage can shape us through genetics is our predisposition to specific health conditions. Many diseases and health conditions have a genetic component, which means that if a particular condition runs in our family, we may be at higher risk of developing it ourselves. For example, if our parents or grandparents have a history of heart disease, we may be more likely to create it ourselves. Similarly, some genetic mutations can increase our risk of developing certain types of cancer.

Our genetic makeup can also influence how we respond to medications. For example, certain genetic variations can affect how our bodies metabolize drugs, affecting their efficacy or the likelihood of side effects. By understanding our genetic predispositions, we can make more informed decisions about our health and well-being. Taking steps to mitigate our risk of specific conditions and making lifestyle choices that align with our genetic predispositions can lead to healthier and happier lives.

Culture and traditions: Besides genetics, our family lineage can profoundly impact us through the culture and traditions passed down from generation to generation. Cultural and religious traditions can play a significant role in shaping our identities and our worldviews. This is particularly true if we come from a family with a strong cultural or religious identity, where specific values and beliefs are deeply ingrained.

Cultural and religious traditions can provide a sense of connection to our family lineage and can help us feel rooted in a larger community. For example, if we come from a family with a strong cultural identity, we may feel a deep sense of pride and belonging to that culture. This can give us a sense of identity and purpose that can be difficult to find elsewhere.

Traditions can also provide a sense of continuity and connection to our ancestors. By carrying on traditions passed down through our family lineage, we can feel connected to our ancestors and the generations that have come before us. This can be a powerful way to honor and remember our ancestors and help us feel a sense of continuity and purpose.

In addition to providing a sense of connection and identity, cultural and religious traditions can shape our beliefs and values. For example, if we come from a family with a strong religious identity, we may have been raised with specific moral and ethical values that are deeply ingrained. These values can influence how we approach the world and guide our decision-making in important areas.

Traditions can also play a role in shaping our sense of community and social connections. For example, if we come from a family with a strong cultural identity, we may have grown up participating in cultural events and celebrations with our extended family and community. These events can provide a sense of connection and belonging to a larger community and can help us build social relationships that last a lifetime.

While cultural and religious traditions can be a source of strength and connection, they can also be a source of tension and conflict. If our beliefs and values are at odds with those of our family or community, this can create tension and lead to isolation or alienation. Therefore, balancing honoring our family lineage and cultural traditions is crucial while making space for our unique identity and beliefs.

Family stories and history: Family stories and history can prove to be beneficial for us to connect with our ancestors and to understand our family lineage better. By learning about the experiences of our ancestors, we can gain a deeper appreciation for the challenges they faced and the triumphs they achieved. This can give us a sense of connection to our past and inspire us in our lives.

Family stories can be passed down through oral traditions from one generation to the next. These stories can offer valuable insights into the lives of our ancestors and can help us better understand the context in which they lived. For example, we may learn about their hardships, such as slavery, displacement, being stripped of their identity, poverty, or war, and how they overcame these challenges. We may also learn about the values and beliefs necessary to our ancestors and how these shaped their lives and decision-making.

In addition to stories, family history can also provide a window into our past. By researching our family history, we can learn about the lives of our ancestors in greater detail. In addition, we may discover exciting facts about our family lineage, such as where our ancestors came from or what professions they had. This can help us feel connected to our ancestors and better understand our identities.

Learning about family stories and history can also be a way to honor and remember our ancestors. By recognizing the struggles and triumphs of our ancestors, we can pay tribute to their lives and their impact on our family lineage. This can be a powerful way to connect with our past and to create a sense of continuity between past and present.

Family stories and history can also provide a way to connect with our relatives and build stronger relationships with our family members. We can create a shared sense of history and identity by sharing stories and information about our family lineage. This can be especially important for families who may have members who are geographically dispersed or who may still need to have the opportunity to spend much time together. Learning about our family lineage can provide a common bond that can help us feel more connected to one another.

Family stories and history can be a rich source of inspiration, connection, and understanding. By exploring our family lineage, we can gain a deeper appreciation for the struggles and triumphs of our ancestors and can create a sense of continuity between past and present. In addition, this can be a powerful way to connect with our family members and develop a sense of purpose and belonging.

Interpersonal dynamics: Interpersonal dynamics within our family lineage can be critical in shaping our personalities and relationships as we grow up. Our families are usually the first social group we are exposed to, and they play a crucial role in shaping our attitudes and behaviors toward other people. Our interactions within our family unit set the tone for how we perceive and interact with others outside of it. If we grow up in a family with a lot of conflict or dysfunction, this can have a profound impact on our ability to form healthy relationships as adults.

Living in a family with many conflicts can be traumatic for children. It can cause them to experience anger, sadness, depression, and fear. Children constantly exposed to conflict can become anxious and have trouble with people or their decisions. As they grow up, they may struggle to maintain close relationships and find it difficult to connect deeply emotionally. They may also find it challenging to communicate their feelings or express them in a healthy manner.

Dysfunctional family dynamics can also impact a child's development of coping mechanisms. Children who grow up in families with high levels of conflict may learn to adapt to that environment in ways that aren't necessarily healthy. For example, they may become very adept at avoiding conflict or may develop a tendency to repress their feelings. This can lead to difficulties in adulthood, such as difficulty setting boundaries, expressing emotions, or avoiding conflict altogether.

Moreover, children who grow up in families with conflict may struggle to develop a sense of self-worth or self-esteem. Children constantly exposed to negative interactions may begin to internalize that negativity and create a negative self-image. This can make it difficult for them to form healthy relationships as adults since they may struggle with feelings of inadequacy, fear of rejection, and difficulty trusting others.

In conclusion, the interpersonal dynamics within our family lineage can significantly impact our ability to form healthy relationships as adults. Living in a family with a lot of conflict or dysfunction can lead to many emotional and psychological issues that can impact our relationships with others. However, it's important to note that there is always time to develop healthy relationship skills. With the help of therapy or counseling, individuals who grew up in dysfunctional families can learn to form healthy relationships and overcome the negative impact of their family dynamics.

Role models: Positive role models are a valuable part of our lives, and family lineage can be a rich source of inspiring individuals who can motivate us to strive for our best selves. By learning about our ancestors' lives, we can better understand our family's values and the legacy they have left behind. Whether it's a grandparent who overcame adversity or a great-grandparent who fought for social justice, their stories can inspire us to pursue our dreams and make a difference in the world.

When we look at the lives of our ancestors, we often find individuals who overcame significant obstacles to achieve their goals. Learning about these people can give us a sense of perspective and help us to see that even the most challenging situations can be overcome with hard work and perseverance. For example, a great-grandparent who emigrated from another country and established a successful business can inspire us to take risks and pursue our dreams. We may also find inspiration in the lives of those who persevered through difficult times such as war, slavery, illness, or economic hardship.

Our ancestors can also provide examples of people who fought for social justice and positively impacted their communities. Learning about these individuals can inspire us to act and work towards creating positive change in our communities. For example, a great-grandparent who was a civil rights activist may inspire us to become involved in local activism or advocacy work.

Furthermore, our ancestors' stories can teach us the values and principles necessary for our family. Understanding their experiences and actions, we can better understand the importance of compassion, resilience, and perseverance. We can also learn about our family's history and culture and how that has shaped our identity.

Our family lineage can provide us with a rich source of positive role models who inspire us to be our best selves and positively impact the world. By learning about our ancestors' lives, we can better understand our family's values and the legacy they have left behind. Their stories can teach us about perseverance, resilience, and the importance of fighting for social justice. We can continue their legacy by following in their footsteps and making a difference in our lives and communities.

In conclusion, our family lineage can profoundly impact who we are as individuals. From genetics to culture, family stories to interpersonal dynamics, the people who came before us have helped shape our identities and experiences. By understanding and embracing our family lineage, we can gain a deeper appreciation for our past and a greater sense of purpose in the present.

Indications of Who Carries Energetic Ancestral Imprints

Repeated patterns, habits, or coping strategies
Family lineage seeks to address energetic imprints passed down through generations. One aspect of family lineage healing recognizes repeated patterns, habits, or coping strategies that may be indications of energetic ancestral imprints.

Many of us may have habits, patterns, or coping strategies we've learned from our families that we repeat without realizing it. These behaviors can be positive or negative, often reflecting the attitudes and beliefs prevalent in our family lineage. For example, if your family has a history of alcoholism, you may have learned coping strategies such as avoiding conflict or suppressing your emotions. Alternatively, if your family has a history of entrepreneurial success, you may have known to take risks and work hard to achieve your goals.

When we see repeated patterns or habits that are negative or self-destructive, it can be an indication of an energetic ancestral imprint. These imprints are often rooted in trauma, such as poverty, war, or oppression, and can be passed down through generations. In addition, these imprints can manifest in our lives in various ways, such as anxiety, depression, addiction, or self-sabotage.

By recognizing these patterns and habits, we can address the energetic ancestral imprints causing them. This can involve a process of healing and releasing these imprints through practices such as meditation, energy work, or therapy. Removing these imprints allows us to free ourselves from negative patterns and behaviors and create a new path for ourselves and our families.

Inherited genetic diseases

There is a growing understanding of the complex interplay between genetics and epigenetics, which can contribute to the development of inherited diseases and may be influenced by energetic ancestral imprints.

Epigenetics refer to changes in gene expression that are not caused by alterations to the underlying DNA sequence but by modifications to the DNA molecule or associated proteins. Various factors can influence these modifications, including environmental and lifestyle factors and energetic imprints passed down through generations.

Evidence suggests that epigenetic modifications can play a role in developing certain inherited diseases, such as cancer, diabetes, and cardiovascular disease. In addition, these modifications can be influenced by factors such as stress, diet, and exposure to environmental toxins, which can be inherited from previous generations.

In family lineage healing, recognizing inherited genetic diseases can indicate the need for energetic healing and the release of imprints that may contribute to these conditions. In addition, by exploring the ancestral history and potential traumas or patterns underlying these conditions, individuals can work towards healing and breaking negative patterns passed down through generations.

Recognizing the potential underlying energetic patterns can be an important aspect of family lineage healing and working towards healing and releasing these patterns.

Abandonment fears & anxiety

Abandonment fears and anxiety can be an indication of energetic ancestral imprints that have been passed down through generations. These imprints can result from unresolved trauma, such as the loss of a parent or caregiver, a family history of neglect or abandonment, or other experiences of disconnection or loss.

When these energetic ancestral imprints are present, individuals may feel a deep-seated fear of abandonment, manifesting in various ways, such as anxiety, avoidance, and codependency. These behaviors and patterns are often rooted in the past and can be passed down through generations, creating a cycle of fear and disconnection that can be difficult to break.

By recognizing these patterns and behaviors, individuals can explore the ancestral history and potential traumas underlying these experiences. This can involve a process of healing and releasing the energetic imprints that are causing the fears and anxiety. Practices such as meditation, energy work, and therapy can be effective in helping to release these imprints and break the cycle of fear and disconnection.

In addition to individual healing, family lineage healing can also be essential to addressing abandonment fears and anxiety. By exploring the ancestral history and patterns passed down through generations, individuals can begin to understand the root causes of their experiences and work towards breaking negative these patterns.

Negative thought patterns

Negative thought patterns can be an indication of energetic ancestral imprints that have been passed down through generations. These imprints can result from unresolved trauma, emotions, and negative thinking patterns passed down through generations.

Negative thought patterns can manifest in various ways, such as self-doubt, self-criticism, pessimism, and negativity. Unfortunately, these patterns are often deeply ingrained and can be challenging or difficult to break, especially if passed down through generations.

This can significantly impact an individual's life, affecting their relationships, career, and overall well-being. However, recognizing these patterns as potential energetic ancestral imprints can be an important first step in healing.

Through individual and family lineage healing, individuals can explore the ancestral history and potential traumas or patterns underlying these negative thought patterns. This can involve a process of healing and releasing the energetic imprints that are causing the negative thoughts and beliefs.

Practices such as Sufi healing, meditation, energy work, and therapy can be effective in helping to release these imprints and break the cycle of negative thinking. Additionally, identifying positive affirmations and cultivating a sense of gratitude can help to reprogram the mind with more positive thought patterns.

Fears and Phobias

It is believed in family lineage healing that fears and phobias can indicate energetic ancestral imprints in a person's family lineage. This belief holds that our ancestors' traumatic or highly emotional experiences can leave an energetic imprint on their descendants, manifesting as fears, phobias, or other emotional and psychological patterns.

According to this belief, these ancestral imprints can be passed down through generations. As a result, they can affect our thoughts, emotions, and behaviors, even if we have no conscious memory of the original trauma. The idea is that by identifying and healing these ancestral imprints, we can release ourselves and future generations from the negative patterns passed down to us.

Many people find value in exploring and healing their ancestral lineage to understand their emotional and psychological patterns better. Whether or not these patterns are directly linked to ancestral imprints, exploring and healing our family history can be a powerful way to gain insight into ourselves and our relationships with others.

PTSD / CPTSD

Post-traumatic stress disorder (PTSD) and Complex post-traumatic stress disorder (CPTSD) are mental health conditions that develop after a person experiences or witnesses a traumatic event. While various factors can influence the symptoms of PTSD and CPTSD, it is believed that ancestral imprints can affect an individual's mental health and well-being, including the development of PTSD and CPTSD. This is because trauma experienced by previous generations can be passed down through the family lineage, resulting in psychological and emotional wounds carried by subsequent generations.

While mainstream scientific research does not support this idea, it is consistent with some family lineage healing practices. These practices emphasize the importance of understanding and healing ancestral wounds to promote individual and collective healing.

It is worth noting that regardless of the cause of PTSD and CPTSD, effective treatments are available to help manage the symptoms and improve overall well-being. These treatments may include psychotherapy, medication, and alternative therapies such as spiritual healing, meditation, and other health and wellness programs. If you or someone you know is struggling with symptoms of PTSD or CPTSD, it is essential to seek the support of a qualified mental health professional.

Experiencing unexplained fears, anger, anxieties, depression, confusion, worries, or behavior.

Psychological and emotional issues can be influenced by traumas experienced by previous generations that have been passed down through the family lineage. As a result, individuals may carry energetic imprints of the traumas and negative emotions experienced by their ancestors. These imprints can manifest as unexplained fears, anger, anxieties, depression, confusion, worries, or behavior that seemingly have no apparent cause or trigger in the individual's life experiences.

However, it is important to note that unexplained fears, anger, anxieties, depression, confusion, worries, or behavior can also be caused by various other factors, including environmental and genetic influences and personal life experiences. Therefore, it is essential to seek the support of a qualified spiritual healer& counselor or mental health professional to identify the root causes of these issues and develop a personalized healing or treatment plan appropriate for the individual's specific needs.

Having hereditary conditions such as addictions

Addictions and other hereditary conditions can be influenced by traumas experienced by previous generations that have been passed down through the family lineage. Individuals may carry energetic imprints of the traumas and negative emotions experienced by their ancestors, which can manifest as hereditary conditions such as addictions. This suggests that unresolved trauma experienced by previous generations can influence the expression of specific genes, increasing the risk of developing addiction and other hereditary conditions in subsequent generations.

Family lineage healing practices emphasize the importance of understanding and healing ancestral wounds to promote individual and collective healing. These practices suggest that by acknowledging and addressing ancestral wounds, individuals can begin to recover from addictions and other hereditary conditions passed down through generations.

Nonetheless, it is important to note that various other factors, including environmental and genetic influences and personal life experiences, can also cause addictions and other hereditary conditions. Therefore, it is essential to seek the support of a qualified spiritual healer& counselor, or mental health professional to identify the root causes of these issues and to develop a personalized protocol or treatment plan that is appropriate for the individual's specific needs.

Feeling stuck and not knowing why or how to get out of it

Feeling stuck and not knowing why or how to get out of it is a common experience. This means that unresolved traumas experienced by previous generations can be passed down through the family lineage and manifest as a feeling of being stuck or limited in life. These energetic imprints can influence an individual's thoughts, emotions, and behaviors, resulting in patterns of self-sabotage or a lack of motivation to pursue their goals and aspirations.

In family lineage healing practices, the importance of understanding and healing ancestral wounds to promote individual and collective healing is emphasized. These practices suggest that individuals can release the energetic imprints that may hold them back by acknowledging and addressing ancestral wounds and finding greater freedom and purpose in life.

However, that feeling stuck or trapped in life can also be caused by various other factors, including mental health conditions such as depression or anxiety and personal life circumstances such as financial or relationship problems. Therefore, it is essential to seek the support of a qualified spiritual healer, holistic or mental health professional to identify the root causes of these issues and to develop a personalized treatment plan that is appropriate for the individual's specific needs.

Having financial constraints

Patterns of financial difficulty can be influenced by traumas experienced by previous generations that have been passed down through the family lineage. This reinforces the idea that unresolved traumas experienced by ancestors can be passed down through the family lineage and can influence an individual's relationship with money and financial success. Energetic imprints of financial struggles can be passed down from generation to generation, manifesting as patterns of financial difficulties, such as persistent debt, low income, or difficulty accumulating wealth.

By acknowledging and addressing ancestral wounds, individuals can release the energetic imprints that may hold them back and find a greater sense of financial abundance and prosperity.

However, financial constraints can also be caused by other factors, including economic conditions, personal financial decisions, and structural inequalities. Therefore, it is essential to seek the support of a qualified financial professional to identify the root causes of financial difficulties and to develop a personalized financial plan that is appropriate for the individual's specific needs.

Overcoming Inherited Trauma

Inherited or intergenerational trauma refers to transmitting traumatic experiences and their effects from generation to generation. This can occur when the trauma experienced by one generation is not fully processed or resolved and is passed down to subsequent generations through cultural and familial narratives, behaviors, and epigenetic changes.

As a holistic approach to healing inherited trauma, family lineage healing can help identify and address patterns of trauma and dysfunction passed down through generations. That is, it can be used to explore one's family history and ancestry, identify patterns of trauma and dysfunction, and work to heal and transform those patterns.

Overcoming inherited trauma can be a complex and challenging process, but several steps can help:

Acknowledge the trauma: Acknowledging the trauma is an essential step in overcoming inherited trauma. It involves recognizing the presence of the trauma and understanding its impact on your life. This may include exploring your family history and identifying trauma and dysfunction patterns passed down through the generations.

For example, if your ancestors experienced war, famine, or displacement, you may be carrying the emotional residue of those experiences in your own life. This may manifest as anxiety, depression, or other forms of emotional distress. By exploring your family history and understanding the experiences of your ancestors, you can begin to make sense of your emotional struggles and gain a deeper understanding of the root causes of your inherited trauma.

Acknowledging the trauma also involves accepting that it is not your fault and that you are not responsible for the trauma your ancestors experienced. In addition, it is imperative to recognize that the trauma is a part of your family's history, but it does not have to define your present or future. By acknowledging the trauma and its impact on your life, you can begin to take steps toward healing and transforming the patterns of dysfunction passed down through the generations.

Seek support: Seeking support from a qualified spiritual healer, counselor or therapist specializing in trauma or lineage healing can be incredibly helpful in overcoming inherited trauma. A trained professional can provide a safe and supportive environment to process your emotions and experiences and offer tools and techniques to help you manage trauma symptoms and improve your overall well-being.

A therapist or counselor can help you understand the impact of inherited trauma on your life and guide you in developing coping strategies to manage difficult emotions and memories. They can also help you explore the root causes of your inherited trauma and work with you to create a plan for healing and transforming those patterns.

Working with a healer, therapist or counselor who specializes in trauma can also help you feel less alone and isolated. They can offer a sense of validation and support and help you build a stronger sense of resilience and self-efficacy.

It is important to note that seeking support from a therapist or counselor specializing in trauma is not a sign of weakness but a courageous step toward healing and transformation. With the guidance and support of a trained professional, you can begin to break the cycle of inherited trauma and create a healthier, more fulfilling life for yourself and future generations.

Practice self-care: Practicing self-care is an essential component of overcoming inherited trauma. Engaging in activities that promote physical and emotional well-being can help reduce stress, improve mood, and promote a sense of resilience and self-efficacy.

Regular exercise is a powerful tool for reducing stress and promoting physical and emotional well-being. Exercise has been shown to improve mood, reduce anxiety and depression, and promote overall physical health. Walking, yoga, or strength training can help you feel more grounded and connected to your body. It can also relieve the release of pent-up emotions and tension. In addition, exercise stimulates the release of endorphins, which are natural mood boosters that can help you feel more positive and energized.

Meditation is another powerful self-care tool for reducing stress and promoting emotional well-being. Meditation focuses on the present moment and can help you develop a greater sense of inner calm and resilience. Even a few minutes of meditation daily can significantly impact your emotional well-being. It can help you develop greater self-awareness and improve your ability to regulate your emotions.

Spending time in nature is also a powerful self-care practice that can help reduce stress and improve mood. Spending time in green spaces has been shown to reduce symptoms of anxiety and depression and promote feelings of well-being. Walking, gardening, or sitting outside in a park can help you feel more grounded and connected to the natural world. It can also promote a sense of calm and inner peace.

Finally, practicing self-compassion is another important self-care practice for overcoming inherited trauma. Self-compassion involves treating yourself with kindness and understanding rather than judgment and criticism. This can include developing self-awareness and learning to recognize and accept your emotions and experiences without judgment. It can help you create a greater sense of self-worth and self-acceptance and promote inner peace and emotional well-being.

Connect with others: Connecting with others who have similar experiences can be an important step in overcoming inherited trauma. This can provide a sense of belonging and validation and help you feel less alone in your struggles. One way to connect with others is to join a support group. Support groups provide a safe and supportive environment where individuals can share their experiences and feelings with others who have had similar experiences. This can help individuals feel heard, understood, and validated, providing a sense of community and belonging. Support groups may be available in person or online and may be led by a mental health professional or a peer facilitator.

Another way to connect with others is to join an online community. Online communities provide a space for individuals to connect with others who have had similar experiences, regardless of location or time zone. This can be particularly helpful for individuals who may live in areas where support groups are not readily available or who may have difficulty leaving their homes due to physical or mental health issues. Online communities may be moderated by a mental health professional or a peer moderator. They may offer a range of resources and support, including discussion forums, chat rooms, and educational materials.

Connecting with others with similar experiences can be an important step in the healing process. It can provide a sense of validation and support and help individuals feel less alone in their struggles. In addition, it can promote feelings of empathy, compassion, and understanding.

Challenge negative beliefs: Inherited trauma can lead to negative beliefs and self-talk, perpetuating a cycle of emotional distress and low self-esteem. These beliefs may include thoughts such as "I'm not good enough" or "I'm destined to fail." Challenging these beliefs and replacing them with positive and empowering thoughts can be a powerful way to overcome inherited trauma and improve emotional well-being.

One way to challenge negative beliefs is to identify them and examine the evidence for and against them. For example, if you think, "I'm not good enough," you might ask yourself, "What evidence do I have to support this belief? What evidence do I have to contradict it?" By examining the evidence, you may see that reality does not support your negative beliefs.

Once you have identified and examined your negative beliefs, you can replace them with positive and empowering thoughts. This may involve developing affirmations or positive self-talk that reinforce your self-worth and self-esteem. For example, you might repeat to yourself, "I am worthy of love and respect," or "I am capable and strong."

Another way to challenge negative beliefs is to engage in activities promoting mastery and accomplishment. This might involve setting goals and working towards them or engaging in enjoyable and fulfilling activities. You can develop a greater sense of self-efficacy and self-worth by focusing on your strengths and achievements.

Developing resilience: Developing resilience is an essential step in overcoming inherited trauma. Resilience is the ability to adapt and cope with stress and adversity, and it can be developed through positive coping strategies.

Positive coping strategies, such as exercise, healthy eating, and social support, can also help you develop resilience. For example, engaging in regular physical activity can improve mood, reduce stress, and increase feelings of well-being. A balanced and nutritious diet can improve overall health and well-being and provide the energy and nutrients needed to cope with stress and adversity. Building positive social connections and seeking support from others can also help you develop resilience by giving a sense of belonging, validation, and support.

By developing resilience, you can better manage stress and adversity and promote emotional well-being. Developing these skills may take time and practice, but you can build strength and overcome inherited trauma with persistence and patience.

Recognizing the Ancestral Story You Were Told

Recognizing the ancestral story you were told is a crucial aspect of family lineage healing. It provides insight into the source of these patterns and helps identify which ones may be holding you back from living a fulfilling life.

Ancestral Stories and Their Transmission

Ancestral stories are narratives, beliefs, and values passed down from generation to generation. They can be explicit, such as family stories or traditions, or implicit, such as unspoken rules or expectations. Ancestral stories can also be influenced by cultural, social, and historical contexts that shape a family's experiences.

Ancestral stories can be transmitted through various means, such as storytelling, family rituals, and cultural practices. In addition, these stories can be passed down consciously or unconsciously, significantly impacting individuals' identity, beliefs, and behavior within a family.

For example, a family may have a tradition of storytelling emphasizing the importance of hard work and perseverance. This story can shape the beliefs and behavior of future generations, encouraging them to work hard and overcome challenges. On the other hand, a family may have a history of trauma that is not explicitly discussed but is transmitted implicitly through avoidance or silence. This can lead to feelings of shame, anxiety, or depression in future generations who may not understand the source of these emotions.

The Impact of Ancestral Stories

Ancestral stories can have a significant impact on individuals and families. They can shape beliefs and behavior, influence relationships and communication patterns, and impact mental health and well-being.

For example, if a family has a history of poverty and hardship, the belief that one must struggle to survive may be deeply ingrained in future generations. This can lead to a mindset of scarcity and fear, which can manifest as financial insecurity, a lack of trust in others, or a reluctance to take risks.

Similarly, if a family has experienced trauma, such as slavery, war or genocide, the emotional wounds can be passed down through generations. This can lead to disconnection from one's culture, a fear of expressing emotions, or a tendency to avoid situations that may trigger traumatic memories.

Recognizing Ancestral Stories for Healing and Transformation

Recognizing the ancestral story you were told is a crucial step in the process of family lineage healing. It involves examining the narratives, beliefs, and behaviors from generation to generation within your family.

By recognizing these ancestral stories, you can understand how they may have impacted your beliefs, values, and behaviors. You may also gain insight into patterns of behavior or issues that have persisted in your family over time.

For example, if you grew up in a family that emphasized the importance of perfectionism, you may have internalized a belief that mistakes are unacceptable. Recognizing this ancestral story can help you understand why you struggle with failure or vulnerability. In addition, it can allow you to challenge this belief and develop a more compassionate attitude toward yourself.

Similarly, recognizing the ancestral story of trauma can help you understand why you may be experiencing symptoms of anxiety, depression, or post-traumatic stress disorder. By acknowledging the source of these emotions, you can develop strategies for healing and resilience, such as therapy, meditation, or support groups.

Recognizing ancestral stories can also help break patterns of behavior that no longer serve you. For example, if your family has a history of conflict or dysfunction, you may have learned communication patterns that are not conducive to healthy relationships. By recognizing this ancestral story, you can develop new communication skills and boundaries that support healthy relationships.

Furthermore, it can facilitate intergenerational healing. It can provide a sense of connection to your family's history, culture, and traditions, which can be empowering and enriching. By understanding and honoring your family's history, you can move forward with greater clarity and purpose and create a legacy that supports future generations.

Ways to Recognize the Ancestral Story you were Told.

There are many ways to recognize the ancestral story you were told.

You can start by exploring your family history and asking questions about your ancestors, such as

What were their experiences?

What were their beliefs and values?

What challenges did they face?

How did they overcome them?

Did you hear stories about your ancestors that emphasized resilience, strength, and perseverance?

Or were there stories that perpetuated negative stereotypes or limited belief about your family's potential?

In addition, you can engage in practices that support healing and transformation, such as therapy, meditation, or journaling. These practices can help you connect with your emotions and beliefs and facilitate letting go of patterns that no longer serve you.

Redrafting Your Ancestral Story

Redrafting your ancestral story is a process of re-examining and transforming the narratives, beliefs, and behaviors passed down through generations within your family and making conscious choices to change them. This process is critical to family lineage healing as it enables you to break free from negative patterns and create a new narrative that supports your growth and well-being.

The Importance of Redrafting Ancestral Stories

Redrafting your ancestral story is a critical step in family lineage healing. It involves re-examining the narratives, beliefs, and behaviors passed down through generations and creating a new record supporting your growth and well-being.

By redrafting your ancestral story, you can challenge negative patterns and beliefs that may hold you back from living a fulfilling life. You can also create a new narrative that aligns with your values and aspirations, empowering you to create a legacy that supports future generations.

The Impact of Redrafting Ancestral Stories

Redrafting ancestral stories can have a significant impact on individuals and families. You can create new narratives that support growth, resilience, and well-being by transforming negative patterns and beliefs.

For example, if a family has a history of poverty and hardship, redrafting the ancestral story can involve re-examining the belief that one must struggle to survive. By challenging this belief and creating a new narrative that supports abundance and prosperity, individuals within the family can experience greater financial security and a sense of empowerment.

Similarly, if a family has experienced trauma, redrafting the ancestral story can involve transforming the narrative of victimhood into one of resilience and strength. By acknowledging the impact of trauma while recognizing the capacity for healing and growth, individuals within the family can develop a sense of connection to their culture and a more extraordinary ability for emotional expression.

Engaging in the Redrafting Process

There are many ways to engage in the process of redrafting your ancestral story. One way is to identify the narratives, beliefs, and behaviors that no longer serve you. This may involve reflecting on your family history and asking questions about your ancestors' experiences, beliefs, and values.

Once you have identified the negative patterns, you can challenge them by creating new narratives that align with your values and aspirations. This may involve engaging in practices that support healing and transformation, such as therapy, meditation, or journaling.

Another way to redraft your ancestral story is to engage in the practice of ritual and ceremony. Rituals and ceremonies can be powerful tools for transforming ancestral stories. They allow you to connect with your ancestors and honor their experiences while creating new narratives supporting your growth and well-being.

For example, if your family has experienced trauma, you may create a ritual that honors your ancestors' resilience and strength while acknowledging the impact of trauma on future generations. This may involve reciting prayers, remembrance, affirmations, lighting candles, or group meditation.

In addition to engaging in personal practices, community-based practices supporting ancestral healing can also be helpful. This may involve participating in cultural events or rituals, connecting with other individuals engaged in family lineage healing, or seeking support from a therapist or spiritual counselor.

Drawing a New Map of the Story for Your Life

Since family lineage healing recognizes that these issues are not solely the result of individual actions or experiences but are often rooted in historical events and family dynamics, healing must involve understanding and addressing the larger context in which these issues arise.

This is where drawing a new map of the story of your life becomes critical. Drawing a new map of the story for your life is a process that involves examining and transforming the narrative of one's life. It is a powerful tool for family lineage healing, as it allows individuals to understand and reframe their personal experiences of patterns of trauma, dysfunction, and hostile behavior that have been passed down through generations in the context of their family history. By understanding these patterns, individuals can transform their narrative and create a new, more positive story for their life.

In the context of family lineage healing, drawing a new map of the story for your life can help us to examine the larger context of our family history and understand the origins of our negative patterns and behaviors. For example, an individual who struggles with anxiety may discover that this pattern has been passed down through generations of their family due to historical trauma or dysfunction. By understanding this context, individuals can break the cycle of negative patterns and create a new, more positive family legacy.

Drawing a new map of your life story can also help heal intergenerational trauma. Intergenerational trauma refers to transmitting trauma from one generation to the next. For example, the trauma experienced by a grandparent or great-grandparent during a war or genocide can profoundly impact their descendants, even if they did not directly experience the trauma themselves. By understanding and healing from this trauma, individuals can break the cycle of negative patterns and create a new legacy for future generations.

Here are some steps to follow:

Begin by reflecting on your life story and identifying key turning points, challenges, and successes. Then, consider how your family history has influenced your choices and experiences and how you have navigated the challenges and opportunities that have come your way.

Use storytelling techniques to explore different aspects of your family lineage. For example, you might write a short story about your great-grandparents and their journey to a new country or create a narrative that explores the cultural traditions and values passed down through your family.

Visualize your family history by visually representing your family tree or a timeline highlighting key events and milestones. You might also use images or symbols to represent different aspects of your family history, such as a photograph of your grandparents or a map of the town where your ancestors lived.

Combine storytelling and visualization techniques to create a cohesive and engaging narrative that tells the story of your family lineage and your life story. For example, you might create a video or multimedia presentation that combines photographs, music, and narration to tell the story of your family's journey through history.

Continuously revise and update your map as you gain new insights and experiences. Your life story constantly evolves, and your understanding of it will continue to deepen. By continually exploring your family history and reflecting on your own experiences, you can create a more nuanced and complex map of your life story that demonstrates the richness and complexity of your identity.

Incorporate the perspectives of other family members into your storytelling and visualization. This might involve interviewing relatives to learn more about their experiences and perspectives or collaborating with family members to create a shared map of your family lineage.

Explore your family history's emotional and psychological impact on your life story. For example, you might use journaling or creative writing to explore how your family's history has influenced your relationships, career choices, or sense of identity.

Use your new map of the story for your life to set goals and make plans for the future. By understanding the forces that have shaped your life, you can more intentionally shape your destiny and make choices that align with your values and aspirations.

Finally, remember that the new map of the story for your life is a work in progress. As you explore your family history and experiences, your understanding of your identity and place in the world will continue to evolve. Be open to new insights and perspectives, and use your map for ongoing self-reflection and growth.

What is Sufism?

With its focus on inner purification, Sufism is a spiritual path that anyone can practice regardless of their religious or cultural background. It is not limited to any particular creed or sect but can be adapted and integrated into any existing belief system. This universal approach is one of the most beautiful aspects of Sufism.

Sufism recognizes many paths to the Divine, and each individual has a unique journey. Therefore, Sufi teachings emphasize connecting with one's inner truth and recognizing the Divine within oneself. This internal connection with the Divine can help individuals find their path and purpose.

Sufism teaches that the heart is the seat of the Divine. Therefore, through spiritual practices such as remembrance of God, meditation, and self-reflection, one can purify the heart and remove any obstacles that prevent one from experiencing the Divine Presence. In addition, this purification process allows the individual to cultivate qualities such as love, compassion, humility, and generosity, which are essential for living a meaningful and fulfilling life.

Sufi teachings also emphasize the importance of serving and treating others with kindness and respect. Sufis believe that by helping others, we serve God and that acts of kindness and compassion can bring us closer to the Divine.

Another critical aspect of Sufism is the spiritual guide or teacher concept. A Sufi teacher can help individuals navigate their spiritual journey and provide guidance and support. The teacher can also help individuals understand and apply Sufism's teachings daily.

In Sufism, the human being is viewed as a microcosm of the entire universe, and the Divine Light of The 99 Names of God is seen as the source of all creation. According to Sufi teachings, these Divine Names can be accessed and channeled by the human being through spiritual practices such as meditation, prayer, and remembrance of God. A person who establishes a strong connection with God can become a channel for the Descent of the Divine Names, which can bring healing and transformation.

The Descent of the Divine Names can profoundly affect a person's physical, emotional, and spiritual well-being. It is believed that the Divine Names carry powerful healing energy that can help to restore balance and harmony to the individual. This healing energy can manifest in different ways, such as reducing pain and inflammation, promoting relaxation and calmness, improving mental clarity, and increasing vitality and energy.

Sometimes, the Descent of the Divine Names can lead to a "major descent," where the healing is so immediate and intense that it can only be described as a miracle. This is a rare occurrence, but it is seen as a powerful testament to the potency of the Divine Names and the transformative power of spiritual practices.

More commonly, the Descent of the Divine Names is experienced as a gradual process, where the person's inner world is gradually cleansed and purified through spiritual practices. This process can help remove any internal obstacles or blockages contributing to the illness or disease. As a result, the person may experience a gradual improvement in their physical and emotional health.

It is important to note that Sufism does not view spiritual practices as a replacement for conventional medicine or other healing systems. Instead, it sees them as complementary approaches that can work together to promote healing and well-being. By establishing a connection to God and channeling the Divine Names, a person can access a powerful source of healing energy that can support and enhance their healing process.

In Sufism, purifying oneself is essential to achieving Union with God, Enlightenment, and the Divine Oneness. This purification involves not only the external actions of a person but also the internal states of their heart, mind, soul, and secret.

The purification process in Sufism is viewed as a science developed and refined over many centuries by enlightened teachers and mystics. This science includes specific steps, practices, and teachings designed to help the seeker overcome their ego and the negative traits that keep them from experiencing a closer connection to God.

One of the critical aspects of this process is the importance of finding a true Guide, or spiritual teacher, who has already walked the path of purification and can provide guidance and support to the seeker. The Guide is essential in helping the seeker navigate the challenges and obstacles that inevitably arise on the spiritual path.

Through the guidance of a true Guide, the seeker can progress through the various stations and steps of purification, which include practices such as prayer, meditation, remembrance of God, and self-reflection. As the seeker progresses, they may experience various spiritual states and insights that deepen their connection to God and bring them closer to the Divine Oneness.

Ultimately, this process aims to reach a state of Unity with God, where the seeker's self is wholly merged with the Divine Presence. This state of Union is seen as the pinnacle of spiritual attainment in Sufism and is believed to bring about a profound transformation in the seeker's being.

Overall, the science of purification in Sufism is a rigorous and transformative process that requires dedication, effort, and guidance. Through this process, the seeker can overcome their ego and negative traits, deepen their connection with God, and ultimately achieve Union with the Divine.

Sufi Prophetic Healing

Sufi Prophetic Healing is based on the fundamental principle that all true healing comes from the Divine and that the human body, mind, and spirit are interconnected and interdependent. Therefore, the Sufi way of healing is gentle, sacred, and practical and seeks to address imbalances and illnesses of all kinds, including physical, financial, emotional, mental, and spiritual.

From the Sufi perspective, illness and imbalances originate in the soul and eventually manifest in our lives. Therefore, the healer in the Sufi way strives to identify the underlying causes of illness and invite sacred, divine light and love to "wash" those areas. This is done through deep spiritual invocations, prayers, and practices derived from the Sufi love, wisdom, and unity tradition.

One of the key elements of Sufi Prophetic Healing is the identification of the "veils" that obstruct the flow of divine energy and light. These veils often result from negative thought patterns, limiting beliefs, or unprocessed emotions buried deep within the soul. In a healing session, the Sufi healer seeks to identify and dissolve these veils through divine love and light.

The healer in the Sufi tradition recognizes that they are merely a vessel through which divine light and love can flow and that all true healing comes from the Divine. This is why spiritual invocations, prayers, and practices are central to healing. These ancient techniques are gentle, clean, comprehensive, and effective in removing veils obstructing the flow of divine energy and light.

Sufi Prophetic Healing also recognizes that transformation must occur in the soul and body for the healing to be complete. This is why Sufi healers emphasize the importance of spiritual purification and growth as part of the healing process. In addition, they help the individual identify and release negative thought patterns, limiting beliefs, and unprocessed emotions and replace them with positive, life-affirming beliefs and emotions.

In addition to spiritual purification and growth, Sufi Prophetic Healing employs various physical and practical techniques to support the healing process. These may include spiritual medicine, natural remedies, dietary changes, and other lifestyle modifications supporting physical health and well-being.

Why Would You Choose Sufi Prophetic Healing?

Choosing Sufi Prophetic Healing can be a personal and individual decision based on one's spiritual beliefs, experiences, and health concerns. Here are some reasons why someone might choose Sufi Prophetic Healing:

Health issues: Sufi Prophetic Healing can be a valuable tool for individuals experiencing health issues or physical illnesses and seeking a holistic approach to healing that addresses their spiritual, mental, and emotional conditions. This approach recognizes that all aspects of our being are interconnected and that imbalances in one area can manifest as physical symptoms in another.

For those who have explored many avenues for healing a physical disease and have not found relief, Sufi Prophetic Healing can offer a new perspective and approach to healing. By identifying the underlying causes of the illness and addressing them at the spiritual and emotional level, this approach can help clear the path to physical healing.

Additionally, for those already receiving treatment for a physical illness, Sufi Prophetic Healing can provide extra support in addressing their condition's mental and emotional aspects. This can help to alleviate stress, anxiety, depression, and other emotional imbalances that can impact physical health.

Financial issues: Sufi prophetic healing can help holistically address economic matters by identifying and addressing the underlying spiritual, mental, and emotional aspects contributing to financial challenges. For example, feelings of fear and anxiety around money can create blockages that prevent abundance from flowing into one's life. By working with a Sufi healer, one can receive guidance and practices to help release these blockages and cultivate a mindset of abundance and gratitude.

Additionally, Sufi teachings emphasize the importance of living in a way that aligns with divine principles, including how one relates to money and material possessions. By cultivating a deeper understanding of these principles and integrating them into one's financial practices, one can experience greater peace, clarity, and abundance in their economic life.

Furthermore, Sufi prophetic healing can help address any karmic patterns or family lineage issues contributing to current financial challenges. By identifying and clearing these patterns, one can experience greater freedom and abundance in their economic life.

Emotional issues: Sufi Prophetic Healing can also benefit those experiencing emotional issues. The spiritual practices and invocations used in Sufi healing can help individuals identify the underlying causes of their emotional distress, such as past traumas, negative thought patterns, or spiritual disconnection. Through the guidance of a Sufi healer, individuals can learn techniques to release emotional blockages and cultivate a deeper connection with their inner selves and the Divine.

For those experiencing depression, fear, or anxiety, Sufi Prophetic Healing can offer a safe and supportive environment to explore these emotions and work towards healing. Through spiritual practices such as prayer, remembrance, meditation, and breathwork, individuals can learn to quiet their minds and connect with their inner source of peace and strength. Sufi healers may also use specific invocations or practices to help release negative thought patterns and emotions contributing to anxiety and depression.

For individuals who have experienced a loss, such as a job, family member, or relationship, Sufi Prophetic Healing can offer support around grief and the healing process. Through prayer, meditation, and other spiritual practices, individuals can find comfort and strength in their faith and connection to the Divine. Sufi healers may also offer guidance on how to honor and process the emotions associated with loss and find meaning and purpose in life after a significant change or transition.

Sufi Prophetic Healing can offer a path toward release and healing for those struggling with forgiveness. Through spiritual practices such as prayer, meditation, and reflection, individuals can learn to cultivate compassion and forgiveness towards themselves and others. Sufi healers may also offer guidance on resisting resentment and anger and moving forward positively.

Lastly, Sufi Prophetic Healing can offer tools and techniques to manage these emotions and find inner peace for those dealing with stress, overwhelm, or uncertainty. Through breathwork, meditation, and prayer, individuals can learn to quiet their minds and find clarity and focus. Sufi healers may also offer guidance on cultivating a deeper connection with the Divine and finding meaning and purpose in challenging times.

Family or relationship issues: Sufi prophetic healing can be a valuable resource for those struggling with family or relationship issues. Family dynamics and relationships can be complicated and challenging, and healing these relationships requires understanding the underlying emotional and spiritual factors contributing to the difficulties.

If you experience isolation and disconnection from important people, Sufi Prophetic healing can help you identify the underlying causes of these feelings and work toward healing and reconciliation. By exploring the emotional and spiritual factors contributing to these feelings, you can better understand yourself and your relationships and build stronger, more meaningful connections with those in your life.

If you struggle with resentment and grudges, Sufi Prophetic healing can help you release these negative emotions and cultivate forgiveness and compassion. In addition, the healing process can help you identify the root causes of your resentment and work towards resolving these issues, allowing you to let go of negative emotions and move towards greater peace and harmony in your relationships.

Finally, if you are struggling with unhealthy patterns in your family or relationships, Sufi Prophetic healing can help you identify these patterns and work towards healing and transformation. By exploring the underlying emotional and spiritual factors contributing to these patterns, you can gain insight into your behavior and the behavior of those around you and work towards building healthier, more fulfilling relationships.

Spiritual issues: Sufi prophetic healing is a powerful tool for those seeking to deepen their spiritual connection with the Divine and address any spiritual issues they may face. One of the main benefits of this healing practice is that it can help individuals reconnect with their spiritual heart and find a sense of purpose and meaning in their lives. This can be especially helpful for those needing help or connection with their spiritual path.

Another key benefit of Sufi Prophetic healing is that it can help individuals deepen their connection to the Divine. Through spiritual invocations, prayers, and practices, individuals can open themselves up to the love and guidance of the Divine and experience a sense of peace, safety, protection, and security in their lives.

For those who struggle with fear or uncertainty, Sufi Prophetic healing can offer a sense of Divine protection, helping individuals to feel more grounded and centered in their daily lives. Healing practices can also help individuals access Divine guidance, especially when facing difficult decisions or challenges.

Finally, Sufi Prophetic healing can benefit those seeking to break through barriers that keep them from living their full potential. By identifying and addressing underlying spiritual issues, individuals can free themselves from limiting beliefs and behavior patterns and move forward with greater clarity, purpose, and confidence.

Sufi Healing Practices

Sufi healing practices are varied and may differ depending on the specific Sufi tradition, lineage, or teacher. However, some common Sufi healing practices include:

Arabic Sacred Letters and Divine Qualities

Arabic Sacred Letters and Divine Qualities are central to Sufi prophetic healing. In Sufi prophetic healing, Arabic sacred letters are considered to have divine power and are used as a tool for healing. Each letter is associated with a specific Divine Quality or Attribute. Combining these letters is believed to create a vibrational energy that can help bring about healing and balance.

The Arabic language is believed to have originated from the Divine and is considered a sacred language in the Islamic tradition. The Arabic alphabet consists of 28 letters, each with a unique shape and sound. These letters are used to write the words of the Quran, considered the literal word of God in Islam.

In Sufi Prophetic healing, the Arabic sacred letters are often written on paper or other materials and used as talismans or amulets to provide protection and healing energy or recited through specific prayers or chants as part of healing practices. The sound of the letters is believed to have a powerful vibrational effect on the body and can help to balance and heal the energy centers.

Arabic sacred letters can also be visualized during meditation or contemplation. By focusing on the shape and sound of the letters, one can connect with the Divine Qualities and access their healing energy. The goal is to align the client's energy with the Divine qualities and activate the body's innate healing abilities.

Sufi healers often use specific combinations of Arabic letters to invoke the Divine qualities and energies needed for healing. For example, the letters Alif, Lam, Mim (A-L-M) are often used in healing because they are believed to represent the Divine Attributes or 99 names of Allah(God)and carry the qualities of Divine protection, guidance, and mercy. Similarly, the letters Ha, Meem (H-M) are associated with the Divine quality of enlightenment and spiritual awakening.

The Arabic letter "Alif" is also associated with the Divine Quality of Unity and is often used in healing practices to help bring about a sense of oneness and connection. The letter "Ha" is associated with the Divine Quality of Life and is used to help bring about vitality and energy.

In addition to the Arabic letters, Sufi healers work with Allah's Divine Qualities (Asma-ul-Husna), Allah's 99 names or attributes. Each Divine Quality represents a unique aspect of the Divine, such as mercy, compassion, forgiveness, and peace, which can be invoked for healing and transformation.

In Sufi Prophetic healing, Arabic sacred letters are often combined with other healing practices, such as energy healing, guided meditation, and prayer. By working with the Divine Qualities and accessing their healing energy through the Arabic sacred letters, one can promote healing and balance on all levels of the being.

Spiritual Invocations

Spiritual invocations are a central part of Sufi healing practices. These invocations are prayers or supplications to the Divine, asking for healing and guidance. In the Sufi tradition, these invocations are believed to be powerful tools for opening the heart and connecting with the Divine and are often recited during healing sessions.

One common form of spiritual invocation in Sufi healing is reciting the 99 Names of Allah, or Asma-ul-Husna, which are Allah's Divine qualities or attributes. Reciting these names is believed to help individuals connect with these qualities and bring them into their lives, leading to healing and transformation.

Another common invocation used in Sufi healing is reciting the Qur'an, the holy book of Islam. The Qur'an is believed to contain healing power, and reciting its verses can help bring about spiritual and physical healing. Some Sufi healers may also use specific verses or chapters of the Qur'an that are believed to have particular healing properties, such as the Surah al-Fatihah, which is often recited for general healing purposes.

In addition to these invocations, Sufi healers may also use other spiritual practices, such as dhikr or remembrance of Allah, meditation, and visualization. These practices are all aimed at helping the individual to connect with the Divine and bring about healing and transformation on a deeper level.

Prayer

Prayer is also a central aspect of Sufi healing practices. Sufism emphasizes the direct personal experience of the divine, and prayer is a means to achieve this connection. Sufi prayer is not just a recitation of prescribed texts but a deepening of one's relationship with God through the heart and the soul.

In Sufism, prayer is seen as a means of healing the body, mind, and soul. It is believed that through prayer, one can access the divine healing power to cure physical ailments, mental disorders, and spiritual imbalances. Therefore, Sufi healers use prayer to facilitate healing in their clients.

One of the critical practices in Sufi prayer is the remembrance of God (Dhikr). Dhikr involves the repetition of the names of God or other sacred phrases, often accompanied by physical movements or breathing exercises. The goal of Dhikr is to quiet the mind and connect with the divine presence within oneself.

Another important aspect of Sufi prayer is the use of music and chanting. Sufi music is believed to heal the mind and body and is often used in Sufi healing ceremonies. In addition, the use of music and chanting helps to create a spiritual atmosphere that facilitates the healing process.

In Sufism, ritual prayers (dhikr) are practice to glorify God and achieve spiritual purification and beautification. Sufis believe prayer can transform the individual and bring inner peace and harmony. Through prayer, one can purify the heart and cultivate virtues such as love, compassion, forgiveness, and gratitude.

The Process of Sufi Healing

The process of Sufi healing involves the assessment and healing of the client along the spiritual/physical energy continuum, as outlined in the steps below:

Connection: Establishing a connection with God is essential to Sufi healing practices. Sufism teaches that God is the ultimate source of healing and that all healing comes from a deep spiritual connection with God. Establishing this connection can take many forms, and Sufi healers often use various techniques to help their clients achieve this state.

One common technique used in Sufi healing is meditation. Meditation involves connecting with the heart and bringing awareness to the center of the chest, focusing on a particular attribute, a sacred phrase, or the name of God. Through this process, the mind surrenders to the heart, which can help to calm the body and create a receptive state for healing.

Sufi healers may also use music or chanting to help their clients establish a connection with God. Sufi music, known as qawwali, is a form of devotional music often used in Sufi healing practices. The music creates a trance-like state to help clients connect deeply and spiritually with God.

In addition to these practices, Sufi healers may encourage their clients to engage in acts of service and charity to connect with God. Serving others and giving to those in need is seen as a way of showing devotion to God and can help to create a sense of connection and purpose in life.

Identification: Sufi healing practitioners believe that illnesses and spiritual imbalances have physical and spiritual causes. Therefore, it is essential to identify the root cause of the problem to heal it effectively. Sufi healers use various methods to identify the needs for healing, healing method, and process, including divination, intuition, and spiritual insight.

One of the most common identification methods used in Sufi healing is divination. Divination involves using tools or techniques to gain insight into the client. For example, they may interpret the client's dreams to gain insight into their subconscious and underlying issues.

Another method used in Sufi healing is intuition and spiritual insight. Sufi healers are trained to cultivate a deep spiritual connection with God, which enables them to perceive the underlying spiritual causes of physical or emotional ailments. This method involves tuning into the client's energy field and sensing any imbalances or blockages causing their symptoms.

Sufi healers may also use the clients' physical examination findings, diagnosis, and medical test results to identify spiritual healing needs. However, they believe that physical symptoms often manifest underlying spiritual imbalances. Therefore, it is essential to address the spiritual causes of the illness to achieve lasting healing.

Once the issue is identified, Sufi healers work with their clients to develop a healing protocol that addresses the illness's physical and spiritual aspects. This may involve healing, prayer, spiritual practices, and recommendations of herbal remedies or dietary changes.

Healing: Sufi healing is a holistic and systemic approach to healing, targeting the whole person, including the physical, emotional, and spiritual aspects of the illness or imbalance. Once the need for healing has been identified through interrogation and divine guidance, Sufi healers use various methods to facilitate healing.

One common method in Sufi healing is natural remedies such as herbs, essential oils, and other plant-based substances. These remedies help balance physical and spiritual symptoms and promote overall health and well-being. For example, herbal remedies may be used to help with digestion, reduce inflammation, or boost the immune system.

In addition to natural remedies, Sufi healers may also use wet cupping or hijama, or various forms of energy healing to promote healing on a spiritual level. Wet cupping helps improve respiratory ailments, provide pain relief, remove toxins from the blood, relieve chronic fatigue, and improve overall health. Energy healing involves working with the client's energy fields to balance and restore them to their natural state of health. This can be done by laying on hands, where the healer places their hands on or near the client's body to transmit healing energy.

Another critical aspect of Sufi healing is using spiritual practices such as dhikr, or remembrance of God, to facilitate healing. Dhikr involves the repetition of sacred phrases or names of God and is believed to help restore the clients' spiritual connection with God. Sufi healers may also use various forms of meditation or visualization to help clients access deeper levels of consciousness and promote healing on a spiritual level.

Sufi healing also emphasizes the importance of lifestyle changes and self-care practices to promote overall health and well-being. This may include dietary recommendations, exercise, stress reduction techniques, and other forms of self-care. In addition, Sufi healers may work with their clients to develop a personalized protocol, incorporating these practices and other forms of therapy, such as natural remedies, wet cupping and energy healing.

It is important to note that Sufi healing is not a replacement for conventional medical care but rather a complementary approach to healing that can be used alongside other forms of treatment. Sufi healers may work with medical professionals to provide a holistic approach to healing that addresses the illness's physical, emotional, and spiritual aspects.

Duration: The duration of Sufi healing practices can vary depending on the nature and severity of the client's condition, as well as the individual needs and circumstances of the client. In some cases, a single session may be sufficient to improve the client's condition significantly. In others, ongoing healings over weeks, months, or years may be necessary to achieve the desired outcome.

Sufi healers typically work closely with their clients to develop a personalized protocol that considers their unique needs, preferences, and circumstances. The protocol may involve a combination of different healing modalities, techniques, and spiritual practices, depending on the nature of the imbalance and the client's needs.

In some cases, Sufi healers may recommend follow-up or ongoing sessions to ensure that the client continues progressing and maintains overall health and well-being. This may involve regular check-ins or adjustments to the protocol based on the client's progress and feedback.

It is important to note that the duration of Sufi healing practices is not necessarily a measure of the effectiveness of the healing. While some imbalances or illnesses may be resolved relatively quickly, others may require ongoing healing and attention over a more extended period.

How to Apply Sufi Practice to Forgiveness

Forgiveness is an integral part of the Sufi healing practice, as it is seen as a critical component of spiritual growth and well-being. Sufi teachings emphasize the importance of letting go of grudges, resentments, and negative emotions, and cultivating inner peace and acceptance, especially when difficult. The practice of forgiveness in Sufi healing is a process of self-discovery and self-transformation, as it involves cultivating a sense of inner peace and compassion. Hence, having a true sense of inner peace entails accepting that the past is the past. This point of acceptance will ultimately allow you to move on.

In the Sufi tradition, seeking forgiveness and guidance can also involve turning to a spiritual teacher or guide. The role of the teacher is seen as essential in helping us to deepen our connection to the divine. A teacher may offer guidance and support as we navigate the challenges of our spiritual path and may help us see more clearly how we have strayed from our true nature.

One way to apply Sufi healing practice to forgiveness is through the practice of dhikr, or remembrance of God. Dhikr involves the repetition of sacred phrases or names of God and is believed to help to restore the client's spiritual connection with God. By focusing on the presence of God and cultivating a sense of inner peace and gratitude, the client can begin to release negative emotions and resentments and move towards a state of forgiveness and acceptance.

Another way to apply Sufi healing practice to forgiveness is through meditation and visualization. Sufi meditation often involves visualization techniques to help clients connect with their inner self and tap into their innate capacity for forgiveness and compassion. By visualizing the person they seek to forgive and sending them loving-kindness and positive energy, the client begins to release negative emotions and cultivate a sense of forgiveness and compassion.

You can also apply the Sufi healing practice to forgiveness through tawba. Tawba helps you seek forgiveness and guidance through reciting prayers or mantras. In the Sufi tradition, there are many prayers and invocations that are believed to help bring us closer to the divine. These prayers may be recited alone or as part of a larger group and can be accompanied by various rituals or practices to help deepen our connection to the divine.

In addition to these spiritual practices, Sufi healing also emphasizes the importance of taking practical steps to facilitate forgiveness, such as having honest conversations with the person who has wronged them, expressing their feelings in a constructive and non-confrontational manner, and working to find common ground and build bridges of understanding.

Conclusion

In conclusion, family lineage healing is a robust multidisciplinary process that allows us to connect with our roots, heal inherited wounds, and fully embody our gifts and potential. By acknowledging and healing our ancestors' patterns, emotions, and traumas, we can create a more fulfilling and authentic life for ourselves and future generations. It's a journey of self-discovery and growth that requires courage, patience, and self-compassion, but it can ultimately lead to greater peace, purpose, and joy.

Family Lineage Healing Scripts

These guided healing meditations are for clearing your family lineage. They may help you release negative patterns or energy that you may have inherited from your ancestors and create space for positive change and growth in your life.

You may record the healing scripts slowly with your voice or another person's voice whom you may feel comfortable with or listen to the recorded scripts on our YouTube channel!

Begin by finding a comfortable position on the floor or a chair. Then, close your eyes and take a few deep breaths in and out, feeling your body relaxed.

Play the recorded healing meditation.

Healing Meditation Script 1

As you continue to breathe, bring awareness to your heart, the center of your chest. Imagine a bright light shining from within your heart, radiating into the world around you.

Visualize your ancestors standing before you as far back as you can imagine.

They may appear as shadows or silhouettes, or you may see them more clearly. Greet them with love and respect, acknowledging the gifts and challenges they have passed you.

Now, imagine a cord of light connecting you to each of your ancestors. This cord represents the energetic connection that you have to your family lineage. Notice the color and texture of the cord. Are there any areas that feel blocked or stagnant?

As you breathe deeply, imagine a beam of pure white light flowing down from the heavens, surrounding you and your ancestors. This light is filled with love, healing, and transformation energy.

Inhale through your nose and exhale through your mouth 7-10 times. With each exhale, imagine releasing negative patterns or energy that you may have inherited from your ancestors. Then, allow the white light to flow through the cord, clearing any blockages or stagnant energy.

As you breathe deeply, imagine a beam of pure white light flowing down from the heavens, surrounding you and your ancestors. This light is filled with love, healing, and transformation energy.

With each exhale, imagine releasing any negative patterns or energy that you may have inherited from your ancestors. Then, allow the white light to flow through the cord, clearing any blockages or stagnant energy.

Now, visualize a beam of light shining down from above, illuminating your family tree. As you look at the branches and leaves of your family tree, imagine that each one represents a person in your family, past or present.

Take a few moments to feel the energy of your family tree.
Notice any emotions or memories that arise........ (Pause). Perhaps you feel a sense of love and gratitude, or maybe you feel a sense of pain or disconnection.
Whatever emotions come up, acknowledge them and allow them to be there. Know that it is okay to feel whatever you feel and that you are in a safe and supportive space........(Pause)

As you focus on your family tree, imagine holding a ball of light in your hands. This ball of light represents all the energy and emotions passed down through your family lineage. It may contain fear, anger, sadness, love, joy, and resilience patterns.

Please take a few moments to feel the weight of this ball of light in your hands........(Pause) and then release it. Then, watch as it rises up and away from you, carrying all the negative patterns and emotions you no longer wish to have.

As the ball of light disappears from view, take a deep breath in and imagine that you are breathing in fresh, healing energy.

Visualize this energy flowing through your body, filling you with light and love........(Pause).

Now, imagine standing at the base of a beautiful mountain.

This mountain represents the strength and resilience of your family lineage. As you look up at the peak, imagine that you can see all of the generations of your family who have come before you. They are standing at the top of the mountain, looking down at you with love and support.

Please take a moment to connect with your ancestors, thanking them for all they have done to bring you to this moment.........(Pause).

Allow yourself to feel their love and guidance, knowing they are always with you.

Now, as you stand at the base of the mountain, imagine that you are holding a basket.

This basket represents all the positive patterns and traits you wish to carry from your family lineage.

Take a few moments to visualize what you want in the basket. Perhaps it is your ancestors' strength and resilience or your parents' love and compassion. On the other hand, it could be a particular skill or talent passed down through the generations.

Whatever you put in the basket, do so with intention and gratitude. Then, feel the basket's weight in your hands, knowing that you are carrying forward the best parts of your family lineage....... chant Ya Karim (O Generous), Ya Halim (O Forebring), Ya Shakur (O Thankful) directly into your heart for 5 to 7 minutes or until you feel it's time to stop without watching the clock.

As you prepare to end this healing meditation, take one final deep breath in, feeling the energy and strength of your family lineage flowing through you. Then, when you are ready, slowly open your eyes, feeling refreshed, renewed, and deeply connected to your family and your inner strength.

Know that you can return to this healing meditation anytime you need to release negative energy or connect with the positive patterns of your family lineage. You are strong and resilient, and you carry the love and support of all those who have come before you.

Healing Meditation Script 2

Family Lineage Healing with the Male Lineage
Welcome to this guided meditation for lineage healing. In this meditation, we will work with the male lineage, going back multiple generations to identify the original ancestor who passed on a pattern, illness, or problem to the descendants. Once we have identified this ancestor, we will have him face the person receiving the healing, cut the cord, and send the ancestor back into the light.

Begin by finding a comfortable seated position. Close your eyes and take a few deep breaths, inhaling through your nose and exhaling through your mouth7 – 10 times. As you exhale, let go of any tension or stress you may be holding in your body.

Now, visualize a bright, white light surrounding you, creating a protective bubble of positive energy. This light will keep you safe as we journey through the generations of your male lineage.

Imagine yourself standing at the entrance of a tunnel. This tunnel represents the gateway to your male lineage. As you enter the tunnel, you feel yourself being pulled back through time, moving through the generations of your ancestors.

As you move through time, notice the patterns and traits that seem to repeat in each generation. Perhaps there is a history of addiction, anger, or depression that seems to run through the male side of your family...........(Pause).

Keep moving through time until you reach the generation where the pattern, illness, or problem first appeared. Take a moment to observe this ancestor and notice any information that comes to you...... *chant gently into your heart.*

Haliiiiim Haliiiiim Haliiiiim Haliiiiim Haliiiiim Haliiiiim Haliiiiim (Forbearing) 7, 11, 33, or 99 times.

Now, imagine yourself standing face to face with this ancestor. As you look into his eyes, you can feel the connection between you. This ancestor has passed on a trait that has affected your life in some way.

Take a moment to thank this ancestor for his gift, as it has helped shape who you are today. However, you are now ready to release this pattern and move forward in a new way.

Visualize a cord connecting you to this ancestor. The cord represents the connection between you and the pattern that has been passed down through your male lineage.

Ask the ancestor if he is willing to cut the cord. If he agrees, imagine a pair of golden scissors appearing in your hand. Gently cut the cord, releasing the pattern that has been passed down through your lineage.......... (Pause).

Now, imagine the ancestor stepping back into the light. As he does so, he takes with him any negative energy or emotions that have been attached to the pattern. This ancestor is now free to continue his journey in the afterlife.

Take a few deep breaths, feeling the release of the pattern from your body............... (Long pause). You are now free to move forward in a new way, without the weight of your ancestors' patterns holding you back.

As you make your way back through the generations, notice how the energy feels lighter and more positive. Each generation that comes after the released ancestor is now free from the pattern, illness, or problem that has been passed down through the male lineage....... chant into your heart Ya Shakur Ya Shakur Ya Shakur Ya Shakur Ya Shakur Ya Shakur Ya Shakur Ya Shakur Ya Shakur (O Thankful) for 3-5 minutes.

When you are ready, slowly bring your awareness back to your physical body. Take a few deep breaths and wiggle your fingers and toes. When you feel ready, open your eyes, and take a moment to ground yourself.

Take note of any shifts or changes that you may feel in the days and weeks following this meditation. You have taken a powerful step towards healing not only yourself but also your entire male lineage.

Testimonials

A year ago ... Dr. Sainfort held an Ancestral Healing Retreat in our facility... Nature's Point Retreat Center in Tygh Valley, OR It was an amazing gathering of women...coming together from across the US to be in the wilds of nature... committing to be here ... receiving this unique multidisciplinary offering of personal healing! Over the course of the retreat with Dr. Sainfort...an uncovering of stuck places surfaced ...much deeper healing happened! Dr. Sainfort holds multiple professional degrees in allopathic medicine, spiritual healing, and body-centered modalities; Dr. Sainfort's deep intuitive assessment and compassionate way of transforming the subtle energy from very deep stuck places was key to my healing. Thank you, Dr. Sainfort...you are a unique, extraordinary healer!
warmly,"
Laila Davis

"I did attend one of the retreats organized by Dr. Sainfort in Sedona, AZ. It was a life-changing experience, one of the best experiences I have ever encountered. During this wonderful journey through Dr. Sainfort's guidance, we were eligible to get to a higher state of spirituality, enlightenment, and self-discovery thanks to her Zen personality full of positivity, love & high spiritual-energetic state. To top it off, the venue was very serene as well. I am definitely looking forward to be eligible to attend another retreat with Dr. Sainfort."
M.E Hajj

"I've had the pleasure to know and be treated by Dr. Sainfort for a few years. Last year, I listened to my heart and life purpose/calling and went to India for the Panchakarma retreat. I'm forever grateful for the assistance provided to me by Dr. Sainfort with the utmost patience, compassion, professionalism, and understanding during my retreat. She provided one on one healing specified to me and group healing. The energy we created was like no other. During my retreat, I was able to focus and work on family lineage, breaking patterns, had various breakthroughs, and, most importantly, the everlasting positive impact I experienced after the retreat I would've never imagined. I left the old me in India and returned as a different woman. I strongly recommend Dr. Sainfort and her services. My family and I are beyond blessed to have crossed paths with her."
Karen

"Dr Sainfort is a loving yet spiritually powerful healer and guide with a wide variety of tools that she makes available to one during their process. I'm immensely grateful for the security I felt to dive deep into my childhood trauma and lineage thanks to Zuleika's keen intuition and close guidance and support. I'm glad to know there are professionals out there willing and equipped to aid in these processes that are extremely relevant and necessary for humanity in these times of ascension. I was blessed to be part of her lineage healing retreat in Vilcabamba, Ecuador"
C. Bermeo

Resources

"An Invitation to Join Dr. Alda Sainfort on one of her Family Lineage Healing Retreats."

Advanced Healing Wellness Center
Visit our website: **www.ahwcenter.com** or
https://advancedhealingwellnesscenter.com/
Email us at info@ahwcenter.com or call us 754-800-2391
Book a private or group spiritual healing / or a family lineage healing session.
Book a Family Lineage Healing Retreat Intensive or Zawiyah (Silent retreat).

Book a Holistic Health Assessment & Evaluation

Book a Panchakarma Therapy (Ayurvedic detox and rejuvenation)

Join our upcoming Family Lineage Healing Retreat

"The Shadow Work Journal" By Keila Shaheen: This shadow work journal provides you easy-to-use pages laying out activities, exercises, journaling prompts, and more.

https://zenfulnote.com

"God's Way" By Dr. Ibrahim Jaffe: Sufi Spiritual Healing Discover the Inner Meaning of Illness and the True Source of Healing.

Institute of Spiritual Healing (ISH)

Offering many programs for learning and deepening the A-PIIR-TB process, as well as understanding and introducing the foundational teaching of Sufism for healing and walking to

https://instituteofspiritualhealing.com
Call 888-237-5233 Ext 1

University of Sufism Programs

Learn to walk to God and traverse the seven spiritual stations leading to awakening and living in the Unity. And become a more advanced Sufi Spiritual Healer.

Sufiuniversity.org
https://sufiuniversity.org
Call 800-238-3060

Follow us

Facebook: ahwcpines

Instagram: @ahwcpines

https://tiktok.com/@advancedhealing

Subscribe to our YouTube channel for more ancestral healing meditation

https://www.youtube.com/@advancedhealingwellnesscen8701

Bibliography

Advanced Healing Wellness Center. "Family Lineage Healing Retreat." https://advancedhealingwellnesscenter.com/family-lineage-healing-retreat/

Amy G. Dougherty. "The Ancestors Within: Reveal and Heal the Ancient Memories You Carry." Brave Healer Productions, 2021.

Ann M. Drake. "The Energetic Dimension: Understanding Our Karmic, Ancestral and Cultural Imprints." O-Books, 2019.

Ariann Thomas. "Healing Family Patterns: Ancestral Lineage Clearing for Personal Growth." Ancestral Wisdom Press, 2011.

Crystal Raypole. "Understanding Intergenerational Trauma and Its Effects." 2022.

https://www.healthline.com/health/mental-health/intergenerational-trauma

Gerald G. Jampolsky, M.D. "Forgiveness: The Greatest Healer Of All." Simon and Schuster, 2011.

Daniel Foor. "Ancestral Medicine: Rituals for Personal and Family Healing." Bear & Company, 2017.

Farhat Naz Rahman. "Spiritual Healing and Sufi Practices." Nova Explore Publications: Nova Journal of Sufism and Spirituality, Vol 2(1), 2014:1-9.

Forough Rafii et al. "Explaining the Process of Spiritual Healing of Critically-ill Patients: A Grounded Theory Study."

Ethiopian Journal of Health Sciences 30(4): 579–588 (Jul 1, 2020).

Howard Brockman. "Dynamic Energetic Healing: Integrating Core Shamanic Practices with Energy Psychology Applications and Process Work Principles." Columbia Press, 2006.

Ibrahim, Jaffe, M.D. "What is Sufism." https://sufiuniversity.org/about-the-university/about-sufism/
_____. "God's Way: Sufi Spiritual Healing." Amazon (Independently published), 2021.

_____. "What is Sufism." https://instituteofspiritualhealing.com/what-is-sufism/

Jamy & Peter Faust. THE CONSTELLATION APPROACH: Finding Peace Through Your Family Lineage." Regent Press, 2015.

Jeanne Ruland & Shantidevi. "Ancestral Healing for Your Spiritual and Genetic Families." Earthdancer Books, 2020.

Kenneth McAll. "Healing the Family Tree." Sheldon Press, 1999.

Kirra K. Swenerton. "Ancestral Lineage Healing." https://rootwisdom.com/ancestral-healing

Lynne Friedman-Gell& Joanne Barron. "Intergenerational Trauma Workbook: Strategies to Support Your Journey of Discovery, Growth, and Healing." Rockridge Press, 2020.

Margaret Ruby. "The DNA of Healing: a five-step process for total wellness and abundance." Hampton Roads Publishing Company, 2006.

Mark Wolynn. "It Didn't Start with You: How Inherited Family Trauma Shapes Who We Are and How to End the Cycle." Viking, 2016.

Peeran S. L. "Sufi Wisdom & Spiritual Consciousness." Authors Press, 2016.

Rebecca L. Hintze. "Healing Your Family History: 5 Steps to Break Free of Destructive Patterns." Hay House, 2006.

Steve Ogan. "Rewriting Your Family History: Principles of Dealing with the Evil Heritage in Your Ancestry." Author House UK, 2013.

Timothy R. Rebbeck et al. "The distinct impacts of race and genetic ancestry on health." Journal of Nature Medicine 28, pages 890–893 (2022).

University of Sufism. "What is Sufi Prophetic Healing?" https://sufiuniversity.org/healingclinic/

_____. "The Loving Power of Forgiveness." https://sufiuniversity.org/sufism/the-loving-power-of-forgiveness/1256/

In Memory of Sidi Muhammed Al-Jamal

Courtesy of Cathy Aisha McCourbrey

What Others say!

"So much Light and knowledgeable practitioners Healing at this center! Highly recommended!"

Mary Halima Fleming

"Dr. Sainfort is tremendous on what she does and services she provides."

Calvin. Griffiths

"Dr. Sainfort is amazing, she truly has a gift of healing. Dealing with grief is not easy but she has started me on a path to find peace. Grateful for her guidance and expertise."

Michelle Munoz

"Knowledgeable, professional, and empathetic way to treat patients in a more natural and holistic approach. Felt better after the first consultation/session of emotional healing."

Perla

"If you are serious about changing your lifestyle then this is the place for you. Great people, great services, and positive vibes 100%."

Enuka Joseph

"The best place on Earth. It has helped me with all the aches and pain that our body takes on a daily basis. Dr Alda goes above and beyond and has changed my life."

Rodolfo Cortez

"I love the Sufism mediation classes. It's brought me closer to my true self and has released pain I've held deep inside."

Cristina Rodriguez

"I'm truly amazed at how fast I got results!"

Madeline Mesa

Made in the USA
Columbia, SC
19 October 2023

24232977R00087